ANTI-PERFECT SO-CALLED HISTORY

A Nation Under God: The Dominican Covenant and My Journey

BY

CAROLINA SANTOS

ACKNOWLEDGMENT

First and foremost, I give all glory and honor to God, whose grace has carried me through every chapter of my life. Without His guidance, strength, and mercy, this story would not exist.

I would like to express my deepest gratitude to my father, whose wisdom, persistence, and unwavering belief in me became a shield in my darkest moments. Even when I did not fully understand his words, they protected and guided me in ways I only came to realize later in life.

To my children, you are the reason I continue to fight, to heal, and to grow. Your love gives my life purpose, and your future is the foundation of my strength.

I extend my appreciation to my family, both near and far, for the lessons, love, and even the hardships that shaped who I am today. Every experience-both painful and beautiful-has contributed to this journey.

To those who have supported me along the way, whether through encouragement, guidance, or simply believing in my voice, thank you. Your presence has made a difference.

I also acknowledge the resilience within myself, the strength to endure, to rise, and to keep moving forward despite adversity. This book is a testament to that journey.

Finally, I dedicate this work to every individual who has ever felt unheard, unseen, or silenced. May this story remind you that your truth matters, your voice is powerful, and your story deserves to be told.

DEDICATION

This book is dedicated to the women who carry the weight of the world on their shoulders.

To the women who work tirelessly, who stay committed to their education, who raise their children with love and strength, even when life offers little in return.

To those who continue to struggle-not because of a lack of effort, but because of broken systems, racism, bullying, domestic violence, abuse, and the absence of proper support.

To the women who have been failed by leadership, overlooked by society, and denied the resources needed to understand their history, their worth, and their power.

This is for the women who rise every day despite exhaustion, despite pain, despite being unseen.

May you find your voice, reclaim your truth, and walk boldly in the dominion God has given you.

You are stronger than the struggle, and your story matters.

About the Author

Carolina Santos is a passionate writer, healthcare professional, and survivor whose life story reflects resilience, faith, and perseverance. Born in the Dominican Republic, she navigated a complex childhood across multiple countries, including Puerto Rico and the United States, shaping her deep understanding of identity, culture, and displacement.

With nearly two decades of experience in healthcare, Carolina has earned multiple certifications, including Nurse's Assistant, Medical Assistant, Phlebotomist, and Medical Billing and Coding specialist. Her dedication to helping others extends beyond her profession, rooted in a lifelong commitment to service, discipline, and personal growth.

Through her work, Carolina explores the intersection of history, faith, and personal struggle, drawing powerful connections between her Dominican heritage, biblical teachings, and real-life experiences. Her writing is driven by a desire to uncover truth, challenge generational cycles, and inspire healing.

A Nation Under God: The Dominican Covenant and My Journey is not just her story, it is a testimony of survival, faith, and the relentless pursuit of truth.

Table of Contents

My Dominican Heritage: A History Forged in Faith and Resilience

My story began in the heat of the Dominican Republic in July of 1987. I did not arrive alone. My twin sister slipped into the world minutes before me, both of us were so tiny that together we barely weighed five pounds. The doctors looked at our fragile bodies, bones wrapped in skin and lungs fighting for breath, and told our parents not to hope too loudly. We were premature, underweight, and according to medical logic, unlikely to survive. But God had already written a different story for us.

Despite the odds, we lived. Not lavishly, not comfortably, but fully. Our infancy and our childhood were made simple, no luxury, no excess, yet we never lacked a meal, a blanket, or the warmth of a family doing the best they could with what little they had. Life in the Dominican Republic felt humble and light in those early years. The sun was always warm, the air always thick with the smell of plantains frying, and the laughter of neighbors drifted through open windows like music. But beneath that softness, there was a shadow, a complicated family dynamic that would shape the rest of our childhood as well as the rest of our lives.

My siblings and I grew up like children caught between worlds. One moment we were in the Dominican Republic, running barefoot through dusty streets, sleeping under our grandmother's roof where love was present, but life was hard. The next moment we were in Puerto Rico, living in the house our father shared with his wife, a place that never quite felt like ours, no matter how long we stayed. And then there were the years in New York, surrounded by our father's family, where the city's noise drowned out the confusion in our hearts but never erased it.

We were children with suitcases instead of stability, always being moved, always being shifted, always being told where home was instead of feeling it.

But the longest stretch of our childhood unfolded in a tiny, almost invisible town in Massachusetts, the kind of place where everyone knew everyone, where winters were long and isolating, and where we learned to adapt to a world that felt nothing like the island that birthed us. It was there, in that small town, that the truth of our situation became painfully clear: we were not being moved for opportunity or love. We were being moved like pieces on a chessboard.

We were pawns in a bitter game of revenge.

My father's decision to take us away from our mother was not a misunderstanding, not a moment of confusion, not a simple custody dispute. It was the physical expression of a deep, festering animosity, a wound between adults that spilled over onto children who had no say, no power, and no understanding of why their lives were constantly uprooted. We were too young to comprehend the motives, but old enough to feel the consequences. The separation from our mother was not just distance; it was a tearing, a ripping away from the one person whose love had never been conditional.

Looking back, I can see how those early years shaped me, the instability, the movement, the emotional tug-of-war. I learned to be strong before I learned to be safe. I learned to adapt before I learned to trust. I learned to survive before I learned to understand.

And yet, despite the chaos, despite the pain, despite the way we were used as leverage in a conflict that was never ours, we survived, just like we survived our birth. Against the odds. Against the predictions. Against the intentions of those who underestimated us.

My story did not begin in comfort or certainty. It began with fragility, in movement, in conflict. But it also began in resilience, a resilience that has followed me through every chapter of my life.

I see now how our past tragedy reflects a global pattern: the use of the innocent to fulfill the vendettas of the powerful. For generations, people—and even nations—have used the Bible as a shield to excuse their darkest behaviors, proving that some stories are as ancient as the text itself. My father came to America in what Dominicans would call a yola; but here in America, we call it banana boats. My father sought the 'American Dream'—the visas, the jobs, and the stability we all crave—but the path to that new life was paved with the same betrayal and displacement that has defined the human diaspora for centuries. I spent my childhood in the Dominican Republic amidst a humble yet complicated family environment. That same hostile environment we also had to live in when we were living in Puerto Rico. While we sought better education and healthcare, the journey was marked by the trauma of a family divided and as 'old as time' struggle for power and survival." While the experiences I had in the US were yet much darker than ever possibly imagined or began to picture. Our biggest challenge was language. Communicating in a new world that systematically already was designed to do exactly that.

Our goal was to learn, not just the American way of life. It was to also learn the American language and its many different Englishes. Upon our arrival we quickly learned just stepping onto the plane alone required us to be able to communicate in an entire world of linguistics and full of language from people around the world, who not only spoke their native language, but also spoke the good English I longed to learn. Though, **At Babel:** God used different languages to **confuse and scatter** humanity because of their pride. Biblical scholars often pair the **scattering at Babel** with the **gathering at Pentecost** (Acts 2), viewing Pentecost as Jesus "undoing" the curse of Babel. **At Pentecost:** After Jesus ascended to heaven, He sent the Holy Spirit, enabling His followers to speak in different tongues so that people from every nation could **understand and be united** in the Gospel.

While the scattering happened in the Old Testament, Jesus is credited with redeeming that diversity in the New Testament—turning what was a tool for confusion into a tool for global salvation. While this occurred thousands of years before the physical birth of Jesus, Christian theology often views this as an act of the **Triune God** (the Father, Son, and Holy Spirit). Many scholars interpret the phrase "Come, **let us** go down" Genesis 11:7 as a reference to the Trinity, meaning Jesus was present and active in this judgment as the eternal Word.

When and why, what Happened?

The Time limit: The event took place sometime after the Great Flood, approximately **4,200 years ago** (around 2200 BC), according to biblical chronologies.

- **The Location:** It occurred in the **land of Shinar** (ancient Mesopotamia, modern-day Iraq), specifically in the city of Babylon.
- **The Reason:** After the flood, God commanded humanity to "fill the earth," but they instead settled in one place to build a city and a massive tower "reaching to the heavens" to "make a name" for themselves. This was an act of pride and rebellion against God's authority.

REASON IS:

As is common for many people, I am immensely proud of the country of my birth and my Dominican heritage. The Dominican Republic possesses a rich and compelling history. From a biblical perspective and beyond imagination, this land, like all others, began with the creation narrative in Genesis. Following the Great Flood, Noah's descendants dispersed across the earth, and it is theorized that some eventually migrated to the Americas.

It was then that I learned in the bible about the tribe of Simeon. And the two brothers that had killed a whole city for the violation of their sister and took the matter of law and justice into their own hands. This is where the Dominicans had descended from. The Tribe of Simeon while, they had been considered the dogs of the lord. Who had helped guard the gates. They had been scattered, fulfilling the prophecy. In the Americas which had included us the Dominicans. Even way back than fighting for the act of the injustice of humanity as whole. While fighting, standing for those who lacked the ability to fight for themselves. And speaking to communicate verbally, for those who can't speak for themselves. To also defend themselves and those who do not have those abilities, against high-ranking families or the most powerful.

The Island of Hispaniola, shared by the Dominican Republic and Haiti, was initially inhabited by indigenous peoples, primarily the Taínos, who arrived around 4000 BC. Their history forms a critical, though often unaddressed, part of the Antilles' past. While direct links between the Taínos and specific biblical events remain unproven today, their story is part of the broader human diaspora—populations scattered from their original homelands. This collective experience of shared geographic, cultural, and ancestral origins is a defining feature of many global communities.

The modern history of the Dominican Republic began with the arrival of Christopher Columbus in 1492. Landing on Hispaniola during his first voyage, Columbus claimed the island for Spain, establishing the first permanent European settlement in the Americas. Spanish colonization led to the exploitation of natural resources and the indigenous population. Disease, forced labor, and conflict drastically reduced the Taíno population.

In the 17th century, buccaneers settled the western part of Hispaniola, which was eventually ceded to the French, becoming Saint-Domingue (modern-day Haiti). The eastern part, Santo Domingo, remained under Spanish control. After a long and bloody revolution, Saint-Domingue declared independence as Haiti in 1804. Santo Domingo declared its own independence from Spain in 1821 and again in 1844, led by national heroes Juan Pablo Duarte, Ramón Matías Mella, and Francisco del Rosario Sánchez.

Despite political instability, economic challenges, and foreign interventions, the Dominican Republic's desire for sovereignty was fierce. A brief period of re-annexation to Spain in 1861 ended quickly when independence was re-established in 1865. The late 19th and early 20th centuries were marked by turmoil and economic dependence on foreign powers, notably the United States, which occupied the country from 1916 to 1924.

Rafael Trujillo ruled with an iron fist from 1930 to 1961. His regime saw economic development alongside utilitarianism and human rights abuses. His assassination in 1961 led to further instability, including a civil war in 1965 and another U.S. military intervention. In the late 20th and early 21st centuries, the nation transitioned to a stable democracy, experiencing significant economic growth, especially in tourism and free trade. Today, the Dominican

Republic is a developing nation rich in agricultural heritage, facing ongoing challenges such as inequality and corruption.

The Size of the Dominican Republic and Its Biblical Connection

- The Dominican Republic is small, impossibly small when you consider the weight of its history, the force of its culture, and the magnitude of its people. On a map, it is a sliver of land in the Caribbean Sea, barely noticeable beside the vastness of the United States, the immensity of South America, or the sprawling continents across the ocean. At just over 18,000 square miles, the Dominican Republic is smaller than many U.S. states, smaller than countries that rarely make global headlines, smaller than the empires that once tried to control it.
- And yet, despite its size, the Dominican Republic carries a presence that feels biblical.
- Its story mirrors the stories of small nations in Scripture, nations overlooked by the world but chosen by God to carry a purpose far greater than their borders. Nations like Israel, a tiny strip of land surrounded by giants, yet central to the entire narrative of the Bible. Nations that were underestimated, invaded, oppressed, and dismissed, yet still rose with a strength that could only be explained by divine intervention.
- The Dominican Republic is one of those nations.
- A Small Nation with a Giant Story
- The Dominican Republic's size has never matched its impact. This small island has endured

colonization, slavery, dictatorship, invasions, economic instability, and natural disasters, yet its people remain some of the most resilient, joyful, and spiritually grounded in the world. The island's smallness has never limited its identity. Instead, it has sharpened it.

- This echoes a biblical truth:
- "God chose the weak things of the world to shame the strong."
- — 1 Corinthians 1:27
- The Dominican Republic is a living example of this verse. A small nation with a loud voice. A small land with a vast soul. A small territory with a global cultural footprint, music, food, faith, language, rhythm, and resilience that reach far beyond its borders.
- The Biblical Pattern of Small Places Becoming Sacred
- Throughout Scripture, God repeatedly uses small places to carry out big purposes:
- Bethlehem, a tiny town, yet birthplace of Jesus.
- Nazareth, a place people mocked ("Can anything good come from there?"), yet home to the Messiah.
- Israel, a small nation surrounded by empires yet chosen to carry God's covenant.

David, the smallest of his brothers yet chosen to be king.

- The Dominican Republic fits this pattern. Its size does not diminish its significance. If anything, it amplifies the miracle of its survival and the richness of its culture.

- Like Israel, the Dominican Republic has been shaped by struggle. Like David, it has fought giants, colonial powers, dictatorships, poverty, and political turmoil. And like the biblical stories, its victories cannot be explained by size or strength alone.
- Land Marked by Dominion and Deliverance
- The very name "Dominican" carries a spiritual echo. Though historically tied to the Spanish word dominico (referring to the Catholic Order of Preachers), the word also resonates with the biblical concept of dominion, the God-given authority to cultivate, protect, and steward the land.
- In Genesis, God commands:
- "Be fruitful and multiply; fill the earth and have dominion…"
- — Genesis 1:28
- Dominican history reflects this calling. Despite being small, the island has produced:
- A culture that multiplies across continents
- A people who carry their identity with pride
- A spiritual resilience that cannot be colonized
- A global influence far beyond what its size predicts
- Dominicans have taken their small land and multiplied its impact across the world, through music, faith, migration, entrepreneurship, and community.
- The Paradox of Smallness and Strength
- The Dominican Republic's size forces a paradox: how can something so small contain so much?
- This is the same paradox found in Scripture:
- A mustard seed is tiny yet grows into a tree.

- A small boy's lunch feeds thousands.
- A small stone in David's sling defeats a giant.
- A small group of disciples transforms the world.
- The Dominican Republic is a mustard seed nation, small in geography, enormous in spirit.
- Its people carry a fire that cannot be measured in miles. Its culture carries a weight that cannot be contained by borders. Its history carries a testimony that mirrors the biblical theme of God using the small to accomplish the extraordinary.
- A Nation Protected by Grace
- For centuries, the Dominican Republic has survived storms, literal and metaphorical, that should have destroyed it. Hurricanes, invasions, political upheaval, economic collapse, and social turmoil have all struck the island, yet it remains standing.
- This survival feels biblical.
- "No weapon formed against you shall prosper."
- — Isaiah 54:17
- The Dominican Republic is proof that a nation's size does not determine its destiny. God's grace does.

The Dominican Republic as a Biblical Echo

- The Dominican Republic may be small, but its story is vast. Its land may be limited, but its people are limitless. Its borders may be narrow, but its influence stretches across oceans.
- In the Bible, God repeatedly chooses the small, the overlooked, the underestimated, not because they are weak, but because their strength reveals His power.

- The Dominican Republic is one of those chosen places.
- A small nation with a giant purpose.
- A tiny island with a biblical heartbeat.
- A land whose size has never defined its destiny, only magnified its miracle

The Dominican Republic as the First Educational and Medical Center of the Americas

The Dominican Republic holds a unique and often under-recognized place in the history of the Western Hemisphere. Long before many nations in the Americas had formal systems of learning or organized medical care, the island of Hispaniola—specifically the territory that would become the Dominican Republic—was the first to build schools, universities, and hospitals. These institutions were not only physical structures but foundations for intellectual life, cultural development, and social organization in the New World. They reveal how the Dominican Republic became the earliest center of education, healing, and human advancement in the Americas.

The First Schools: The Birth of Learning in the New World

Education in the Americas began on Dominican soil. As early as the first decades of the 1500s, Spanish missionaries and administrators established schools to teach reading, writing, religion, and governance. These early classrooms were created for both Spanish settlers and Indigenous Taíno communities, making the island the first place where European-style education was introduced to the hemisphere.

The arrival of the Dominican Order (the Order of Preachers) played a crucial role. Known for their intellectual tradition, the Dominicans built structured learning environments that went beyond basic instruction. They emphasized philosophy, theology, and the humanities, planting the seeds of higher education long before other colonies even imagined such institutions. This early commitment to teaching made the Dominican Republic the birthplace of formal schooling in the Americas.

The First University: A Center of Knowledge for the Entire Hemisphere

In 1538, the island achieved something monumental: the founding of the Universidad Santo Tomás de Aquino, the first university in the Americas recognized by a papal bull and royal decree. This institution—located in what is now Santo Domingo—became the intellectual heart of the New World.

Modeled after the great universities of Salamanca and Alcalá in Spain, it offered advanced studies in theology, law, philosophy, and medicine. It trained priests, lawyers, administrators, and scholars who would go on to shape colonial society across the Caribbean and Latin America. The university symbolized more than academic achievement; it represented the Dominican Republic's role as the first center of organized knowledge in the hemisphere.

While other countries later built their own universities, none can claim the historical primacy of Santo Domingo. The Dominican Republic was the first to institutionalize higher learning, setting the standard for academic life in the Americas.

The First Hospitals: Healing and Human Care Begin in Santo Domingo

Just as it pioneered education, the Dominican Republic also became the first territory in the Americas to establish hospitals. The Hospital San Nicolás de Bari, founded around 1503, is widely recognized as the first hospital in the New World. Built in Santo Domingo, it served as a place of healing for colonists, Indigenous people, and enslaved Africans alike.

This hospital was more than a building—it was a symbol of organized medical care. It introduced European medical practices to the hemisphere and provided structured treatment at a time when most of the world still relied on informal or home-based remedies. Its ruins still stand today as a reminder of the Dominican Republic's early leadership in public health.

Alongside San Nicolás de Bari, other medical institutions soon followed, including charitable houses and infirmaries run by religious orders. These facilities created the first medical network in the Americas, proving that the Dominican Republic was not only a political and economic center but also a humanitarian one.

A Legacy That Shaped the Americas

The Dominican Republic's early development of schools, universities, and hospitals shaped the trajectory of the entire hemisphere. These institutions:

- Introduced structured education to the New World

- Created the first generation of American scholars and administrators

- Established organized medical care centuries before modern health systems

- Set cultural and intellectual standards that influenced neighboring colonies

This legacy is often overshadowed by later historical events, but it remains a foundational truth: the Dominican Republic was the first cradle of learning and healing in the Americas.

Conclusion

To understand the Dominican Republic is to recognize its pioneering role in the history of the Western Hemisphere. Long before independence movements, modern governments, or contemporary nations existed, the island was already shaping the future of the Americas through education and medicine. Its early schools, its groundbreaking university, and its first hospital reveal a nation that has always been at the forefront of human development. The Dominican Republic was not simply a colony—it was the birthplace of knowledge, culture, and care in the New World.

- Why is this connection to my history, my Dominican Heritage, and the Bible so important to me?
- Before the Puerto Ricans Arrived: The Forgotten Dominican Presence in America's Earliest Forced Labor Camps
- Long before the Dominican flag ever waved in Washington Heights, and long before Puerto Ricans migrated to New York in the great waves of the 20th century, there were Dominicans already on American soil—not as immigrants, but as the earliest enslaved labor force brought from the first colony of the New World. Their presence is buried under centuries of silence, but the truth is carved into the earliest history of the Americas.
- The Dominican Republic—then called Hispaniola—was the first point of European colonization in the hemisphere. It was the first place where Indigenous Taíno people were enslaved by the Spanish, and the first place where Africans were forcibly transported to replace the Indigenous population devastated by disease and exploitation. This system of forced labor began in the 1490s, when the Spanish Crown granted settlers land and enslaved Indigenous people to work it. From this island, the Spanish exported not only sugar, gold, and tobacco—but also human beings.
- Dominicans in Early American Labor Systems
- When the Spanish expanded into North America, they brought with them enslaved laborers from the

16

Caribbean, including from Hispaniola. These early enslaved people—Indigenous and African—were moved through Spanish trade routes into what would later become the United States. The Caribbean, especially Hispaniola, was the training ground for plantation systems that would later dominate the American South and its economy. Sugar and tobacco—two crops that shaped the destiny of millions—were first cultivated by enslaved laborers in the Caribbean before being transplanted into North America.

- This means that Dominicans—through their Indigenous and African ancestors—were part of the earliest waves of enslaved labor long before Puerto Ricans ever set foot in the United States. Puerto Rican migration to the mainland did not begin in significant numbers until the early 1900s, after the island became a U.S. territory. But Dominicans, through forced displacement, were present centuries earlier.
- Enslaved Caribbean Labor in New York's Tobacco Industry
- New York is rarely imagined as a slave state, but it was. In the 1600s and 1700s, enslaved labor—much of it originating in the Caribbean—was used in New York's tobacco farms, docks, and urban households. The plantation system that shaped the American South also influenced northern colonies, where enslaved people worked in agriculture, shipping, and early manufacturing.

- Caribbean-born enslaved people were especially valued because they already had experience with plantation labor. Many were trafficked through Caribbean ports before being sold into New York. This included people from Hispaniola, whose forced labor history began earlier than any other colony in the hemisphere.
- Dominicans in Hawaii's Sugar Plantations
- Centuries later, another wave of Caribbean laborers—including Dominicans—were brought to the far edges of the American empire: Hawaii. Sugar plantations in Hawaii relied heavily on imported labor from across the world, including the Caribbean, after the abolition of slavery. These plantations were modeled after the Caribbean sugar system, which had been perfected through centuries of forced labor on islands like Hispaniola.
- Dominicans, along with other Caribbean workers, were recruited or coerced into these brutal labor contracts. They cut cane under the same sun that had burned their ancestors in the Caribbean, carrying with them a legacy of survival that stretched across oceans.
- A Legacy Buried but Not Erased
- The story of Dominicans in America did not begin with the migration boom of the 1960s. It began in the 1500s, when the island of Hispaniola became the first laboratory of slavery in the New World. It continued through the forced movement of enslaved Caribbean people into New York's early economy. It stretched

all the way to Hawaii, where Caribbean labor shaped the sugar empire of the Pacific.

- Dominicans were here before the Puerto Ricans.
- Dominicans were here before the United States was even a country.
- Dominicans were here because they were taken— enslaved, displaced, and erased from the narrative.
- This is not a simple historical line. It is a spiritual and cultural echo, a chain of ideas stretching across continents and millennia.
-
- The First Laws: Ur and the Birth of Human Order
- Long before the Dominican Republic existed, long before the Bible was written, the ancient city of Ur, located in modern-day Iraq, produced some of the earliest known legal systems. These early Sumerian laws were established:

Connecting my History, my Faith, and my Personal Identity

The history of La Navidad, the first European settlement established in 1492 and named for Christmas, and the founding of Santo Domingo (the oldest continuous European city in the Americas, founded by Columbus's brother in 1496), underscores the nation's deep Catholic roots. Dominican Friars, such as Bartolomé de las Casas, famously condemned the Spanish treatment of the natives, arguing from a Christian basis that the indigenous peoples were children of God.

This complex history sparked my desire to connect the history of my country, the history of Christianity, and my own personal history and culture. My central question is: How much does history truly repeat itself? Wars, world conflicts, and persecution seem cyclical. Are these patterns solely political, or do they follow generational blood lines? What might some call a generational curse? I want to explore how war, inflation, taxes, Christianity, and family trauma all intersect and follow a family's bloodline and heritage.

The Power of the Flag:

I come from the only country in the world with a Bible on its flag, placed directly in the center. The Bible is open to John 8:32: "Y conoceras la Verdad, y la Verdad nos hará libres" (You will know the truth, and the truth will set you free). Above the Bible are the words "Dios, Patria, y Libertad" (God, Homeland, and Liberty), the national motto, of the Dominican Republic.

This is more than a verse; it is a declaration. Dominican freedom was not given; it was fought for with faith in one hand and courage in the other. The flag's colors also carry meaning: Blue for liberty, white for salvation, and red for the blood of Jesus Christ and our people.

Learning this inspired me to study the Bible more closely. I wanted to know where Dominicans were mentioned in scripture. This journey of this discovery felt necessary given my background and achievements. I graduated from high school with high honors and scholarships. I was the top ROTC student for four years, completed National Guard training, and earned seven healthcare licenses (Nurse's Assistant, Home Health Aide, Medical Assistant, Phlebotomy, MedTech, Medical Billing and Coding, and EMR electronic medical records). I took college courses in Anatomy, Physiology, Psychology, Biology, and Chemistry. I also took college courses from criminal justice, state and local governments as well as business entrepreneurship and business math. I worked in healthcare for almost 20 years... Yet I had still never read the bible entirely from cover to cover.

My Dominican Heritage: Blood, Faith, and a Search for Truth

As mentioned previously, I am fiercely proud of my Dominican heritage. The Dominican Republic is as rich as its tremendous, wild story—a history rooted in biblical narratives and human resilience. As we get into more details about my country, its history, as well as its biblical connections.

Like all lands, our island of Hispaniola was part of the Genesis creation story. After the flood, Noah's descendants migrated across the earth, eventually reaching the Americas. Hispaniola was home to the Taínos, indigenous people who arrived around 4000 BC. Their history, shared with Puerto Rico, is a painful part of an "Anti-Perfect So-Called History" that many still refuse to address today. While direct biblical links aren't evident, we are all part of the broader human diaspora—populations scattered from their homelands but connected by shared origins.

Our recorded history begins with Christopher Columbus in 1492. He landed on Hispaniola and claimed it for Spain, establishing the first permanent European settlement in the Americas. Spanish colonization was brutal; forced labor and disease decimated the Taíno population. In the 17th century, buccaneers settled the west, which became French Saint-Domingue (Haiti), while the east remained Spanish Santo Domingo.

After Haiti declared independence in a bloody revolution in 1804, Santo Domingo fought for its own freedom. We declared independence from Spain in 1821, and finally regained it in 1844, thanks to Juan Pablo Duarte, Ramón Matías Mella, and Francisco del Rosario Sánchez.

Our nation faced constant turmoil. Incredibly, the Dominican Republic agreed to go back under Spanish rule in 1861, a short-lived mistake that lasted only four years. The "Anti Perfect" forces of the "Anti Perfect Dogs of the Lord" came hard, as we reestablished our independence in 1865. The late 19th and early 20th centuries brought political chaos and U.S. intervention (1916-1924).

Then came Rafael Trujillo, who ruled with an iron fist from 1930 to 1961, bringing both development and immense suffering. His death led to civil war and another U.S. intervention in 1965. Today, we are a developing democracy, thriving in tourism and agriculture, while still battling inequality and corruption.

Connecting the Past to My Present

The founding of the first European city, Santo Domingo, by Columbus's brother in 1496 established the Dominican Catholic order. Friars like Bartolomé de las Casas famously condemned the mistreatment of the Tainos, arguing for their humanity based on Christian faith.

This history drove me to connect my country's past, Christianity, and my own life. My burning question is: Does history repeat itself? Are we living through generational curses, or just the inevitable cycles of conflict? How do wars, inflation, taxes, Christianity, and family trauma all connect through a bloodline and heritage? Are we feeling the traumas of the past? And how are there intersecting for centuries?

My history pushed me to look at the connections between My country's past, Christianity, and my own life, and it raises deep questions about whether history truly repeats itself or whether we are simply caught in long-standing cycles of conflict. It makes me wonder if what we call generational curses are really the lingering effects of wars, inflation, taxes, and trauma that have shaped families for centuries. These forces—spiritual, economic, political, and emotional—often pass through bloodlines, influencing how people think, survive, and respond to the world. In many ways, we do feel the weight of the past, because the struggles of previous generations leave marks on culture, faith, and identity that continue to intersect and shape us today.

The Genesis: Origins and the First Inhabitants

Like all lands formed by the Creator, the island of Hispaniola was birthed in the narrative of Genesis 1:1, "In the beginning God created the heavens and the earth." Before the maps were drawn, this land was known to God.

The Taínos, who arrived around 4000 BC, were the first stewards of this paradise. While history books call this migration, the Bible speaks of the Diaspora—the scattering of peoples. As Acts 17:26 tells us, "From one man he made all the nations, that they should inhabit the whole earth; and he marked out their appointed times in history and the boundaries of their lands." The Taínos were part of this divine appointed, children of Noah's lineage spreading to the ends of the earth.

However, we also see the tragedy of human condition. The arrival of Christopher Columbus in 1492 brought the collision of worlds. The first settlement, La Navidad (The Nativity), was named after the birth of Christ, yet the history that followed was far from holy. The exploitation of the Taínos and the importation of slaves mirrors the suffering found in Lamentations 5:2-5: "Our inheritance has been turned over to strangers... We labor and have no rest."

This era birthed what I call the "Imperfect History"—a time of pain, forced labor, and disease. Yet, even in this darkness, there was a light. The Dominican Friars, led by Bartolomé de las Casas, stood up as the conscience of the church. He argued, using the very scriptures the conquerors claimed to follow, that indigenous people were children of God. He embodied Proverbs 31:8: "Speak up for those who cannot speak for themselves, for the rights of all who are destitute."

The Struggle for Sovereignty: A Biblical Cycle

The history of the Dominican Republic reads like the book of Judges—a cycle of oppression, crying out to God, and deliverance.

1600s-1800s: The island was torn between Spanish and French control (Saint-Domingue), leading to the birth of Haiti and the complex relationship between our two nations.

1844 Independence: The liberation from Haitian rule was not just a political event; it was a spiritual declaration. Our founding fathers—Juan Pablo Duarte, Ramón Matías Mella, and Francisco del Rosario Sánchez—understood that true freedom requires a spiritual foundation.

This is why the Dominican Republic is the only nation in the world with the Holy Bible at the center of its flag.

The Bible is open to John 8:32: "Y conoceras la Verdad, y la Verdad nos hará libres" ("And you shall know the truth, and the truth shall set you free").

The Motto: Dios, Patria, y Libertad (God, Homeland, Liberty). This order is intentional. God comes before the Homeland. As Psalm 33:12 says, "Blessed is the nation whose God is the Lord."

The Colors:

Blue (Liberty): Represents the heavens and God's protection (Psalm 19:1).

White (Salvation/Peace): Represents the cross and sacrifice

(Isaiah 1:18).

Red (Blood): Represents the blood of our heroes, and ultimately, the blood of Jesus Christ (Ephesians 1:7).

The Era of Iron and Fire: Generational Curses?

My research led me to a difficult question: Does history repeat itself because of politics, or is it a spiritual cycle?

We saw the brief re-annexation to Spain (1861-1865), the US occupations (1916-1924, 1965), and the iron-fisted rule of Rafael Trujillo (1930-1961). Trujillo's era was one of "utilitarianism" "building the economy while crushing the human spirit. The Bible warns of such leaders in Proverbs 29:2: "When the righteous thrive, the people rejoice; when the wicked rule, the people groan."

This repetition of trauma—wars, rumors of wars, inflation, and instability—forces me to ask about Generational Curses.

Exodus 20:5 speaks of the sins of the fathers being visited upon the children.

But Ezekiel 18:20 promises that "The son shall not bear the iniquity of the father."

The trauma in our bloodlines is real, but so is the cure. The trauma stops when a generation decides to seek the Truth mentioned on our flag.

My Personal Exodus: Breaking the Cycle

This brings me to my own story. I looked at my heritage—the resilience of the Taíno, the faith of the friars, the courage of the Trinitarians—and I realized that I am the product of this survival.

I asked, "What is my place in this?" Jeremiah 29:11 answers: "For I know the plans I have for you, declares the Lord, plans to prosper you and not to harm you, plans to give you hope and a future." Disciple only means disciplined one. Yet we always heard for years that God gives his hardest battles to his strongest soldiers.

I did not just survive; I prepared for battle:

Mental Discipline: Graduating high school with honors and representing Massachusetts high school students of highest honors for three years was my way of applying 2 Timothy 2:15: "Study to show thyself approved unto God, a workman that needed not to be ashamed."

Military Service: Four years of ROTC and two years of National Guard training taught me discipline, echoing Psalm 144:1: "Praise be to the Lord of my Rock, who trains my hands for war, my fingers for battle."

The Ministry of Healing: Earning seven healthcare licenses—CNA, HHA, Medical Assistant, Phlebotomy, MedTech, Medical Billing & Coding, and EMR—was not just for a career. It was a call. Like that of a Good Samaritan, I spent nearly 20 years in healthcare, serving the broken. I mastered Anatomy, Physiology, and Chemistry biology and psychology because I wanted to understand the "fearfully and wonderfully made" body described in Psalm 139:14.

The Truth That Sets Us Free

I started this journey by asking if we were living out the traumas of the past. The answer is found in the center of my flag. We are not bound by the "Anti-Perfect" history of man; we are liberated by the Truth of God.

The Dominican Republic's history is a testament that freedom is not given; it is fought for with faith in one hand and courage in the other. My life—my education, my service, my licenses—is the continuation of that fight. I am not just a descendant of the Diaspora; I am a living testimony of Philippians 4:13: "I can do all things through Christ who strengthens me."

I carry the blood of the Taíno, the fire of the revolution, and the seal of the Bible on my flag. The cycle of trauma ends with me; the cycle of blessing and healing begins now.

The Dominican Republic's Contribution to Modern Law and Its Biblical Roots

The very first laws were created 5,000 years ago. Laws had originally emerged with the institutions of property, marriage, and government. The very first written laws were approximately 3000 BC and had been found on clay tablets among the ruins of Ur. Which is one of the city states of Summeria.

Connecting Dominican History, the Bible, Hammurabi's Code, and the Laws of Ur

Dominican history is a story of collision, Taíno roots, African endurance, and Spanish conquest, all converging on one island to create a people whose identity is carved from survival, faith, and reinvention. To understand the Dominican Republic's spiritual and cultural DNA, I had to research far beyond the Caribbean. I must trace the idea of law, dominion, and identity back to the ancient world, to the first written laws in Ur, to the monumental Code of Hammurabi, and to the biblical narratives that shaped the worldview of the colonizers who brought Christianity to Hispaniola.

- Property rights

- Marriage rules

- Social hierarchy

- Penalties for wrongdoing

These laws were humanity's first attempt to impose order on chaos, a theme that later appears in Scripture.

The Bible itself begins with God imposing order on chaos in Genesis 1. Dominion, the right to rule and steward creation, is given to humanity:

This idea of dominion becomes the foundation for all later law codes, including those that shaped the ancient Near East.

Hammurabi's Code: The First Great Legal Monument

The Code of Hammurabi, written around 1750 BCE, is one of the earliest and most complete legal codes ever discovered. It established:

- Justice

- Retribution ("eye for an eye")

- Social order

- Rights and responsibilities

Many scholars note similarities between Hammurabi's laws and biblical laws in Exodus and Deuteronomy.

Hammurabi:

Bible:

This does not mean the Bible copied Hammurabi. Instead, both emerged from the same ancient Near Eastern legal culture.

These early legal systems shaped the world that eventually shaped Christianity, which in turn shaped the Spanish colonizers who brought the Bible to the Dominican Republic.

The Dominican Republic: A New People Formed by Old Laws

When Spain colonized Hispaniola, they brought:

• Roman law (descended from earlier Near Eastern law traditions)

• Biblical law

• Catholic theology

These systems were built on foundations laid thousands of years earlier in Ur and Babylon.

Dominican society was shaped by:

• Spanish legal codes

• Catholic moral law

• African communal traditions

- Taíno cultural memory

The result was a person whose identity was forged through law, faith, and survival.

Biblical Themes in Dominican History

Dominican history mirrors biblical stories in striking ways:

Exodus, Liberation from Oppression

Africans enslaved in the Caribbean lived their own version of Exodus. They saw themselves in Moses, in Israel, in the God who frees the oppressed.

Joseph, Rising from Suffering

Dominicans have repeatedly rebuilt themselves after suffering, colonization, dictatorship, poverty, echoing Joseph's rise from slavery to leadership.

Esther, Courage Against Tyranny

The Mirabal Sisters mirror Esther's courage. They stood against Trujillo the way Esther stood against Haman.

Ruth, Loyalty and Rebuilding

Dominican women, especially, embody Ruth's resilience, rebuilding families and communities through loyalty and sacrifice.

The Spiritual Thread Connecting It All

From Genesis to Hammurabi to Dominican history, one theme repeats:

Dominion, the right and responsibility to shape the world.

- In Genesis, dominion is God-given authority.

- In Hammurabi, dominion is legal order.

- In Ur, dominion is the first attempt at civilization.

- In the Dominican Republic, dominion is survival, identity, and cultural power.

Dominicans inherited dominion not through bloodlines, but through struggle.

Their dominion is:

- African resilience

- Taíno memory

- Spanish religion

- Biblical faith

- Cultural creativity

It is the dominion of people who refuse to be erased.

A People Formed by Ancient Echoes

The Dominican Republic is a young nation built on ancient foundations. Its culture, laws, and spirituality carry echoes of:

- The first laws of Ur

- The justice of Hammurabi

- The stories and commandments of the Bible

- The resilience of African ancestors

- The endurance of Taíno survivors

- The faith of Spanish colonizers

Dominican identity is a living intersection of these worlds, a testament to how ancient ideas of law, dominion, and justice continue to shape modern people.

While the Dominican Republic today follows a Civil Law system (based on the Napoleonic Code) rather than the Common Law system used in the US and UK, the events that took place on its soil made a monumental contribution to the Universal Human Rights laws that govern the entire world today.

The "common" standard of human dignity used in international law was arguably born in Santo Domingo.

The Birth of International Human Rights Law (1511)

The very first public cry for human rights in the Americas happened in Santo Domingo. In 1511, the Dominican friar Antón de Montesinos delivered a sermon that shook the Spanish Empire. He questioned the legal right of colonizers to abuse the indigenous Taíno people.

The Contribution: This sermon sparked the legal debates in Europe (the School of Salamanca) that created International Law. It established the idea that "rights" are not just for Christians or Europeans but are inherent to all humans by nature.

The Biblical Backing: Montesinos opened his sermon with John 1:23: "I am the voice of one crying in the wilderness." He used this to declare that he was the voice of Christ in the "wilderness" of the New World, calling the lawless actions of the colonizers into judgment.

The "First Advocate" of the Americas: Bartolomé de. las Casas

Bartolomé de las Casas, a priest in the Dominican Republic (then Hispaniola), is often called the father of the anti-slavery movement and a pioneer of modern humanitarian law. He argued that the natives were rational beings with souls and rights that the King could not violate.

The Contribution: His writings directly influenced the "New Laws" of 1542, which were the first legal attempts to protect indigenous rights. These concepts of "natural rights" eventually evolved into the modern Universal Declaration of Human Rights used by the UN today.

The Biblical Backing: Las Casas was convicted by Sirach 34:21-22 (Ecclesiasticus), which reads: "The bread of the needy is the life of the poor; whoever deprives them of it is a man of blood. To take away a neighbor's living is to murder him; to deprive an employee of his wages is to shed blood." This scripture convinced him that the economic exploitation of the Dominican Republic's original inhabitants was not just "business," but biblical murder.

The Flag: A Legal Declaration of Truth

The Dominican Republic is the only nation in the world with a specific Bible verse cited as a core symbol of its national identity and freedom. This serves as a unique contribution to the concept of sovereignty based on divine truth.

The Contribution: The flag establishes that the nation's liberty is legally and spiritually dependent on "The Truth." In a legal context, this mirrors the courtroom's requirement for truth to achieve justice. Many do not know this; but placing your hand on the bible. To say the truth and nothing;

but the truth in courtrooms around the world derived from concept in the capital of the Dominican Republic a city named Santo Domingo.

The Biblical Backing: The Bible at the center of the flag is open to John 8:32: "Y conoceras la Verdad, y la Verdad nos hará libres" ("And you shall know the truth, and the truth shall set you free"). This connects the legal concept of "liberty" (freedom from tyranny) directly to the spiritual So, while the Dominican Republic didn't write the British "Common Law," it provided the moral and spiritual spark for the Human Rights laws that now supersede all other laws in the civilized world. Talk about an anti-so-called perfect history.

Another anti-so-called perfect history is carried in the Dominican music that is not just a collection of rhythms, it is the island's heartbeat, pulsing through centuries of survival, resistance, and reinvention. To understand Dominican music is to peel back the layers of the nation's identity, to feel the tension between joy and struggle vibrating through every drumbeat, every guitar string, every voice that has ever risen from the island's soil. It is a history written not in textbooks, but in sound, raw, rhythmic, and uncontainable.

When Africans were violently brought to the Caribbean, they carried with them complex polyrhythms, spiritual drumming traditions, and communal dance structures. These traditions fused with Taíno and Spanish elements, creating the foundation for all later Caribbean genres, including the Cuban son, the direct ancestor of salsa.

Dominicans were part of this fusion from the start because Hispaniola was the first point of colonization, the first site of African arrival, and the first Caribbean crucible where these musical worlds collided.

The Dominican Pulse Inside Salsa's Origins

While Cuba is widely recognized as the birthplace of son, the genre that later evolved into salsa, Dominicans were already shaping the Caribbean soundscape that fed into it. Dominican music evolved from the same Indigenous and African roots, producing genres like merengue and palos, which share rhythmic structures, percussion patterns, and call-and-response forms with early Cuban music.

Dominicans migrated throughout the Caribbean, including to Cuba and Puerto Rico, carrying their rhythms with them. Caribbean ports were not isolated; they were musical highways. Dominican musicians, workers, and sailors contributed to the cross-island exchange that shaped early Afro-Caribbean music.

By the time salsa began taking shape in the 20th century, Dominicans were already part of the musical bloodstream of the region.

New York City: Where Salsa Exploded, And Dominicans Were Already There

Salsa as a named genre took form in New York City in the 1940s–1970s, when Caribbean migrants, Cubans, Puerto Ricans, Dominicans, Panamanians, and others, blended their musical traditions in the barrios of Harlem and the Bronx.

Dominicans were part of this early migration wave. They worked in factories, bodegas, and clubs, and they brought their own musical instincts into the jam sessions, dance halls, and street parties where salsa was being born.

Even though Cuban and Puerto Rican musicians dominated the record labels, Dominican musicians and audiences were part of the ecosystem that made salsa a movement, not just a sound.

And as salsa grew, Dominicans shaped it directly:

• Dominican percussionists brought güira and tambora-influenced playing styles into salsa bands.

• Dominican dancers added footwork and body movement rooted in merengue and Afro-Dominican traditions.

• Dominican communities supported salsa clubs, radio stations, and record shops that kept the genre alive.

Dominicans were not outsiders to salsa, they were contributors, innovators, and cultural carriers.

The Unshakable Dominican Influence

Modern scholars and cultural critics now recognize that Dominicans helped shape salsa's identity, especially through rhythm, percussion, and working-class expression. Salsa was born from the streets, from struggle, from migration, and Dominicans lived that story alongside their Caribbean siblings.

Salsa's heartbeat, the layered percussion, the communal call-and-response, the spiritual undertones, echoes the same Afro-Taíno legacy that defines Dominican music.

Dominicans didn't just join salsa later.

They were part of the ancestral fire that made salsa possible.

✊ A Raw, Powerful Truth

Salsa is not just Cuban.

Not just Puerto Rican.

Not just New York.

It is Caribbean, born from the first island that felt the weight of colonization, the first island where African drums met Indigenous chants, Hispaniola.

Dominicans were there at the beginning of Caribbean music.

Dominicans were there when Afro-Caribbean rhythms crossed borders.

Dominicans were there in New York when salsa exploded.

Dominicans are still there today, shaping, dancing, and redefining the genre.

To claim Dominican presence in salsa is not to erase others, it is to restore what history tried to blur: that the Dominican people have always been part of the Caribbean's musical genesis, from the first drumbeat to the global stage.

It begins long before colonization, in the humid air of the Caribbean forests where the Taíno people carved their world out of earth and spirit. Their music was not entertainment; it was ceremony. The maracas rattled like seeds shaking inside a gourd, the güiro scraped with a rasping whisper that sounded like the island breathing. These were the first sounds of Quisqueya, organic, earthy, pulsing with life. Though much of Taíno culture was violently erased, their rhythmic fingerprints remain embedded in Dominican sound, like faint ancestral echoes that refuse to disappear.

Then came the ships, heavy, wooden, and carrying the weight of a brutal new world. Enslaved Africans were forced onto the island, but they brought with them something colonizers could not chain: rhythm. Their drums were not instruments; they were lifelines. The palos and atabales thundered at a depth that felt like the earth itself was speaking. These rhythms carried grief, defiance, prayer, and memory. They were the heartbeat of people who refused to be spiritually broken. Even today, when those drums sound during religious festivals, and any celebration for gatherings, they vibrate with centuries of survival.

Spanish colonizers layered their own musical traditions onto this growing cultural fusion. Guitars arrived, bright, melodic, and delicate, contrasting sharply with the deep, grounded African percussion. The Spanish brought romance, ballads, and European structure. But the island transformed these influences, bending them into something new, something distinctly Dominican.

Out of this collision of worlds emerged merengue, the genre that would become the Dominican Republic's national identity. Born in the rural countryside, merengue was the music of farmers, laborers, and everyday people. It carried the dust of the fields, the sweat of long days, the laughter and sorrow of community life. Its rhythm was fast, urgent, and alive, a blend of African syncopation, Spanish melody, and Caribbean soul. By the 20th century, merengue had become a cultural force, pulsing through dance halls, radios, and political propaganda alike. It was the sound of a nation claiming itself.

But Dominican music did not stop evolving. In the shadows of bars and brothels, in the neighborhoods the elite pretended not to see, another genre was being born, bachata.

It was raw, emotional, and unpolished. The guitars wept, the bongos throbbed, and the lyrics bled heartbreak. Bachata was the voice of the poor, the wounded, the longing. For decades it was dismissed as vulgar, low-class, unworthy. But music has a way of rising, and bachata rose with vengeance. By the 1990s and 2000s, there were new artists who transformed it into the global phenomenon that it is today. What was once marginalized became a symbol of Dominican pride around the world.

And then came the new generation, loud, unapologetic, and electric. Dembow exploded from the streets with a relentless beat that felt like adrenaline in musical form. It was the sound of youth, rebellion, and digital-age identity. Fast, repetitive, and infectious, dembow became the soundtrack of Dominican urban culture. Alongside it grew urban merengue, reggaeton fusion, and a wave of experimental genres that blended tradition with modernity.

Yet even as Dominican music evolves, the old rhythms remain. The palos, salves, and atabales still echo in religious ceremonies. Merengue still fills dance floors. Bachata still breaks hearts. Dembow still shakes car speakers and street corners. Dominican music is not a timeline, it is a living organism, constantly shifting but always rooted in the island's history of resilience.

To study Dominican music is to study the Dominican soul, a soul shaped by colonization, resistance, joy, pain, faith, and unbreakable creativity. It is a story told through rhythm, a history carried in sound, and a legacy that continues to evolve with every generation.

Origins of Christianity and the Prophetic Destiny of the Dominican Republic

The following timeline details the historical birth of Christianity and traces the spiritual and prophetic connections that link the Bible to the Dominican Republic—a nation whose very existence and symbols are deeply intertwined with scripture.

The Detailed Origins of Christianity (1st Century AD)

Christianity did not begin as a European religion; it began as a Semitic movement in the Middle East, which is critical to understanding the "Diaspora" concept I had mentioned earlier.

30-33 AD (The Foundation): Christianity emerged in the Roman province of Judea (modern-day Israel/Palestine). It was founded on the life, death, and resurrection of Jesus of Nazareth.

The Event: The pivotal moment was Pentecost (Acts 2), occurring 50 days after the Passover, where the Holy Spirit descended on the Apostles, empowering them to speak in different tongues. This marked the birth of the "Church."

33-100 AD (The Apostolic Age):

Peter and James led the church in Jerusalem.

Paul the Apostle (formerly Saul) played the crucial role of taking the faith to the "Gentiles" (non-Jews), spreading it across Asia Minor, Greece, and Rome. This fulfilled the prophecy in Isaiah 49:6: "I will also make you a light for the Gentiles, that my salvation may reach to the ends of the earth."

313 AD (Legalization): For three centuries, Christians were persecuted. This ended when Emperor Constantine issued the Edict of Milan, legalizing Christianity. By 380 AD, it became the official state religion of the Roman Empire.

The Arrival in the Americas (The Dominican Connection)

The history of Christianity in the Western Hemisphere began in the Dominican Republic. It is the "Cradle of Christianity" for the Americas.

1493 (The Arrival): On Christopher Columbus's second voyage, he brought 12 missionaries to Hispaniola.

January 6, 1494 (First Mass): The first Catholic Mass in the New World was celebrated at La Isabela, on the northern coast of the Dominican Republic.

1496 (First Baptism): The first Indigenous person to accept the faith in the Americas was the Taíno chief Guaticaba, who took the baptismal name Juan Mateo. He later became the first martyr of the New World for the faith, famously saying "Dios naboria daca" ("I am the servant of God") before his death.

Biblical Prophecies & Connections to the Dominican Republic

While the words "Dominican Republic" do not appear in the Bible, theologians and believers have long traced specific prophetic threads that point to this nation. These connections center on the "Islands," the "Name," and the "Flag."

The Prophecy of the "Islands of the Sea"

The Hebrew prophets often spoke of the "isles" or "coastlands" (Hebrew: Iyim) that would wait for God's law. Many believers interpret these verses as a prophetic reference to the Caribbean and the Americas, which were unknown to the prophets but known to God.

Isaiah 24:15: "Therefore in the east give glory to the Lord; exalt the name of the Lord, the God of Israel, in the islands of the sea."

Connection: This verse is widely cited by Caribbean theologians as a direct mandate for the Dominican Republic. The "East" often refers to the origins in Jerusalem, while the "Islands of the Sea" refers to the expansion of the Gospel to the uttermost parts of the earth.

Isaiah 42:4: "He will not fail nor be discouraged, till he has established justice on the earth; and the coastlands shall wait for His law."

Connection: The Dominican Republic literally "waited" for the law of God, and when it gained independence, it placed that Law (the Bible) directly at the center of its identity.

Isaiah 60:9: "Surely the islands shall wait for Me, and the ships of Tarshish first, to bring your sons from afar..."

The Prophetic Name: "Dominican"

The country is named after Saint Dominic de Guzmán (Santo Domingo), the founder of the Dominican Order (the Friars).

The Pun on the Name: In Latin, the Dominican friars were often called Domini Canes, which translates to "The Dogs of the Lord" or "The Hounds of God." Many people don't know where the name bounty hunter and its profession originated from. The term "bounty hunter" in which comes from the word "bounty," meaning a reward paid to someone for capturing a person or recovering something valuable, and it became widely used in English-speaking countries when private individuals were hired to track fugitives for money. While the Dominican Republic didn't use the exact English term, the same idea existed throughout Dominican history, especially during Spanish colonial rule, when rewards were offered for capturing escaped enslaved people, rebels, or criminals. Later, during the Trujillo dictatorship, the government relied on paid informants and trackers to hunt political opponents, which functioned much like bounty hunting even though it wasn't called that. Similar reward-based systems also appeared along the

Dominican-Haitian border, where civilians were sometimes paid to capture smugglers or rebels. These patterns show that although the Dominican Republic didn't use the English name "bounty hunter," the practice of paying people to pursue others has deep roots in its history. In which arrived far beyond the Taino Caribbean Islands.

The symbolism: This aligns with the idea of being "Watchdogs" for God's truth, this "Anti-Perfect" power (the fierce defense of truth) was seen in friars like Montesinos and De Las Casas who "barked" at the Spanish Empire to stop abusing the Taínos. They were the "Hounds of God" protecting the sheep (the people). The Covenant of the Flag (The Only One in the World)

The most direct link between the Bible and the Dominican Republic is the Flag, which acts as a visual prophetic scroll.

The Verse (John 8:32): "Y conoceras la Verdad, y la Verdad nos hará libres."

This is a conditional prophecy. It says freedom is not just physical (breaking chains); it is spiritual (knowing the Truth/Jesus). By placing this on the flag in 1844, the Founding Fathers (La Trinitaria) entered a national covenant. They declared that the nation's freedom depends entirely on its adherence to God's truth.

The Cross: The white cross that divides the flag represents Peace and Sacrifice. It divides the red (blood of war) and blue (liberty), symbolizing that peace only comes through the Cross of Christ.

The Trinity: The secret society that formed the nation was called "La Trinitaria" (The Trinity). The nation was literally born in the name of the Father, Son, and Holy Spirit.

The Prophetic Lineage

Genesis: The land is formed.

Isaiah (700 BC): Prophecy that the "Islands of the Sea" will glorify God (Isaiah 24:15).

1492 AD: The Gospel arrives but is corrupted by human greed (The "Imperfect History").

1511 AD: The "Dogs of the Lord" (Dominicans) bark for justice (Montesinos' sermon), aligning the land with God's justice.

1844 AD: The nation is born and seals its destiny with John 8:32 on the flag, fulfilling the prophecy that the "coastlands would wait for His law."

I am not just a citizen of a country; historically and spiritually, I am a citizen of the only nation on earth that has legally bound its existence to the Word of God's concept of "truth" (the Gospel). Directly at the center of its existence and even today is the only flag in the entire world. Something I had begun to be reminded of myself of in my daily life.

Legal Concept   Origin in DR History Biblical Foundation

Universal Human Rights Montesinos' Sermon (1511) in Santo Domingo demanding justice for Taínos.   John 1:23 ("Voice in the wilderness")

Labor Rights & Justice Bartolomé de las Casas arguing against forced labor (encomiendas). Sirach   34:22 (Depriving wages are bloodshed)

Sovereignty & Liberty the National Motto and Flag design (1844). John 8:32 (Truth sets you free)

The Prophecy of a Father and the Silence of the Law

For years, I treated my father's advice like a joke. My siblings and I would laugh at his warnings, finding humor in his delivery despite the gravity of his words. He saw the rot in my marriage long before I was willing to admit it. He warned me that the family I had married could never hold any loyalty to me. He saw it clearly the day my husband stole 189 of my father's prescribed narcotics—medication he desperately needed for his arthritis. When I confronted my husband, he told me to "mind your business" with a venom that should have signaled the end.

My father, even with his limited English, understood the trajectory of my life better than I did. He told me that if I didn't leave soon, I would lose everything I had spent almost twenty years building. He warned me that they would "use me bone-dry" and then discard me to keep my children. For both income and secret animosity. At the time, it sounded like an impossible, "funny" exaggeration. I was a CNA working overnights and a Medical Assistant during the day. While taking a few college courses in the morning after work. Although I was the financial, emotional, and physical pillar of the home, even as I was being abused in every way a person can be—physically, mentally, emotionally and sexually while being drained financially.

Between my grueling work schedule and studying for my nursing degree at our local community college, I had no time to breathe, let alone defend myself. I was living like a single parent in a home, while learning to raise a grown man, even spending my rare days off caring for my husband's grandmother because his aunt—who was being paid by the state to care for her—did nothing. Amidst this exhaustion, my father took me to Boston to apply for my citizenship test. "Do something, I cannot do because of the language," he pleaded. "Stop laughing. One day, you will call and thank me for this."

That day came in March 2017.

I had just finished a 16-hour double shift at the nursing home, my body and mind pushed to the limit. I walked into my home to find my husband high and drunk, having spent the day fighting about my new car, like as if he was the one paying for it. He had seen a message on my Facebook from a friend of my father— In his drug-fueled paranoia, he began to beat me in front of our young children. After almost 20yrs of this behavior daily before and after work or school. I finally got tired of getting abused. If he was not beating me, yelling at me cheating on me stealing my money, my cards to take more money out or making sure I was knocked after a long shift to take off in my car. I tried all around the border. For the first time in my life, my soul broke. I dialed 911, believing that in America, the police were a sanctuary.

But when the sirens arrived, the "American Dream" turned into a nightmare. My husband, a 6'4", 300-pound man, began to cry hysterically. He told the officers that *I* had strangled him and suffocated him in his sleep. He claimed my bruises were from being drunk and falling. He knew exactly how to use his fluent English and his "spoiled only child" charm to manipulate the narrative.

Despite the physical impossibility—I am 4'11" and 120 pounds—the police believed him. As the red and blue lights flashed at 4:00 AM, I was placed in the back of a cruiser. I watched my children crying through the window, wondering if I would ever see them again. In my state of shock and exhaustion, my English failed me. I tried to explain that he was attacking me, but the police report twisted my words, claiming I admitted to an assault. It did not help that his mother also talked to the police and had told them she'd witnessed the act. She claimed my children couldn't verify the story because they too were too traumatized at what their mother had done. While his father had claimed to the police. That it had been the both of us enacting an abusive behavior daily in their home.

I spent numerous amounts of days in a Jail cell, shivering in the cold, surrounded by the smell of urine and the scuttle of insects. In that cell, I was given two sheets of toilet paper at a time and treated like a monster and a high-level criminal. While I sat there, my mother-in-law had accepted my husband's new girlfriends in her home instantly and was already at Walmart buying new sheets for my bed, clearing out as many of my belongings as she could fit into the trunk of my car. Seventeen days later, both a new woman, and a couple known friends was living in what I thought was our home, being called "stepmothers" by my children. Living at no cost, what had cost me so much physically, mentally, emotionally and most importantly financially, and beyond what any words can ever explain.

In the darkness of that cell, my father's "funny" words stopped being a joke. They became my lifeline. *Gracias, Papi,* I whispered. If he hadn't forced me to get my citizenship, I would have been deported to my country, that I haven't known since I was a small child. Because I listened to him just enough to secure my legal status, I am still here able to fight for my children and their stability. Even though my husband had stolen the money I had saved twice. That third time was the charm, and I managed to obtain my citizenship. For the sake of my children, securing my legal status to stay was highly important. I do consider this to be close to my kids and a blessing overall.

I had spent nearly 9 years fighting to get my children back. I have climbed out of homelessness by translating the very resources my father gives me from Spanish to English. I am still struggling to be heard, still struggling to make the system understand the truth behind the language barrier. I realized that my father's "embarrassment" about his English wasn't a weakness—it was a shield he was trying to pass to me. I am here now, nurturer, daughter, and mother, refusing to be silenced by a story that was written for me by someone else. I am finally ready to speak my own truth.

To connect my own personal life story of betrayal, the "language barrier" used as a weapon, and my father's prophetic warnings to the Bible, I looked to the themes of False **Accusation**, **The Joseph Narrative**, and the **Power of the Tongue.**

The Spiritual Battle of the Truth

My father's warnings were not just the advice of an old man; they were a spiritual discernment of a **reaping and sowing** that I couldn't yet see. I thought his words were "funny" because I lacked spiritual eyes to see that I was being set up for a "pit experience," much like **Joseph in the book of Genesis**.

The Weapon of False Accusations

When my husband cried wolf to the police, claiming a woman half his size had overpowered him, he was walking in the spirit of Potiphar's **Wife**. In **Genesis 39**, she grabbed Joseph's garment and lied to the authorities, saying he had attacked her. Joseph, like me, was innocent and lacked the "language" of power to defend himself against a high-ranking family. And of those of people of power. He was thrown into a dungeon based on a lie, just as I was thrown into jail.

The Language Barrier and the "Confused Tongues"

I spent my life mastering English, yet in the very moment of my own greatest need, the system acted like the **Tower of Babel (Genesis 1:1)**. My words were "confused" and twisted by the police. The Bible says in **Proverbs 18:21**, *"Death and life are in the power of the tongue."* My husband used his tongue to bring death to my reputation and my home, while my own tongue—stuttering in trauma—could not find the words to save me.

But my father understood a different principle. He knew that the **Holy Spirit** was the Great Translator. He pushed me to get my citizenship because he knew a time would come when my legal status would be the only thing protecting me from being "scattered" or (deported). Even though as an American citizen I had always felt like my father scattered or deported me from my country. Either way the overwhelming feelings of not belonging were and still is to remain within me today.

The Prophecy of the Father

My father's persistence mirrors **Proverbs 4:1**, *"Listen, my sons, to a father's instruction; pay attention and gain understanding."* I laughed at him, but his words were a hedge of protection. When I sat in that cell for numerous days, smelling the urine and feeling the cold, I realized that

God was using my father as a **Watchman on the Wall (Ezekiel 33:6)**. Because I had finally listened to the watchman and secured my citizenship, the "enemy" could take my house and my bed, but they could not take away my right to stay and fight for my children.

The Restoration

When I spoke about the story of the "new sheets" and the "new stepmothers" moving in after only 17 days felt like the work of the Devourer. But the Bible promises in **Joel 2:25**, *"I will restore to you the years that the swarming locust has eaten."*

My 20 years of healthcare experience, my seven licenses in healthcare, and my struggle through homelessness are my "wilderness years." Like Job, who lost his children and his health but refused to curse God, I am learning that the truth is directly on my on my flag—**John 8:32**—is not just a slogan. *"The truth shall set me free."*

The truth isn't just about speaking English correctly; it's about the fact that God saw what happened at 4:00 AM. He saw the drugs, the theft of the narcotics, and the bruises on my body, and the many physical and sexual assaults. My constant over working to be the sole provider for my family and so many in my husband's family. He watched me run for my life for over 7 years. Getting shot at whether I held my children in hand or not. Paying for the drug debts of my husband. Though never having the acknowledgment of knowing how to use any drugs I still paid so hard for it. He seen the fear in me holding my babies while being pointed in the face with guns holding my babies to dear life not knowing where my husband was even located. He saw fear in my heart when he almost drowned me on the boat in the middle of the ocean as my entire life flashed past me. He watched me turn how much I can tolerate from my husband physically, mentally, emotionally, financially and even sexually and the other types of abuse from others around me like that of friends and family members of mine and my husband's family as a means of my definition as well as the of meaning of love, loyalty and my ability to forgive, yet the unforgivable. I am fighting for my children today because I am standing on **Isaiah 54:17**: *"No weapon formed against you shall prosper, and every tongue which rises against you in judgment You shall condemn."*

My father arrived in America with an "embarrassment" of his language, but he installed within me a legacy of survival. I was a "naive child" and a young black Latina woman who became a victim of an ancient revenge, but through the "funny" words of my Papi and the grace of the Bible, I am being rebuilt. I am no longer consider the severity of a laughing joke; I am a witness to the fact that you can be silenced by a language, but you are never silenced by the Truth.

This is my story of a "dark night of the soul," where betrayal and systemic injustice converged during a season of global isolation. After being the sole provider and helped many with a place to live. Now I am sleeping alone at parks and roof tops in hopes to feel safe. Fought everyone's battles with them and acted as a refuge for all family and friends. Now it is my turn, and I have just me and a higher power to find any type of mental stability inside of myself. Those numerous months of darken isolation and drunkenness with an over stimulated and uncontrollable sorrow just crying. Like that of the loud cry of the people of Egypt. I was experiencing my own pain that caused my great cry of mourning. Like that of the Passover and the 10th plague and the death of the first born. It was the same outcry and grief as my mental instability that had gotten me such a hard time getting out of. That terrible feeling of loneliness. While yet having to accept that the women I thought where my friends were now living in Polly relationships with my husband. Showing my young daughters that though they were raised calling them an aunt. That they are now mutual stepmothers. While confusing the mind of the young. My young daughters watching these women kissing each other, touching each other in inappropriate places. Sparked many questions, confusions and not understanding and wondering if it was normal. Having to accept the very family members I had been too good too for too many years. Using my situation against me and making up stories about me possibly being abusive to them too. Having my children rehearsed what is going to be said to the courts next. While I had full acknowledgement and understanding of knowing. That even the closest to me will say anything to use my children to get back at me for the things I hadn't committed yet. Hiding my children during severe situations in which their mother was needed. Just to keep me worried, sick to my stomach and call it even knowing deep inside yet, again I had done nothing to them but be there when no one else was. Now being too good to be true to too many friends and family have and is so unusual and rare that it is also considered HYPICROSY OR FAKENESS within an individual.

The Valley of Deep Shadows

During a time of global isolation, the weight of personal hardship felt particularly heavy. Separated from my children and facing accusations, a period of deep sadness and struggle ensued. Challenges included navigating financial difficulties, dealing with legal issues, and confronting complex family dynamics. The experience was marked by a sense of being unfairly treated and facing obstacles in trying to rebuild myself and move forward.

Biblical Parallels: Finding my own Story in the Word

This journey mirrors several figures in the Bible who faced false accusations, financial hardship, and deep despair. In which I felt Had connections to my story, the story of my country as well as the bible.

The Betrayal of Laban (Genesis 31)

Like facing financial obstacles and challenges with resources, Jacob worked for Laban, who constantly changed his wages and deceived him. Genesis 31:7 says, *"your father has cheated me by changing my wages ten times."* God eventually saw the injustice and restored Jacob, just as there is a promise for restoration.

The False Accusations Against Joseph (Genesis 39)

Joseph was falsely accused and thrown into prison for a crime he didn't commit. He sat in the darkness of a dungeon while others forgot him, yet Genesis 39:21 reminds us: *"But the Lord was with Joseph and showed him steadfast love and gave him favor."*

The Spirit of Heaviness (Psalm 34 & 88)

Times of deep sadness and struggles are reflected in the raw honesty of the Psalms. Psalm 88:6 describes feelings of being in a low place: *"You have put me in the lowest pit, in the darkest depths."* Though is not like I had stopped believing in Jesus, the lord God, or the holy spirit. But I do have to admit I felt like God had left me. Yet, the Bible promises that God is *"close to the brokenhearted and saves those who are crushed in spirit"* (Psalm 34:18).

Breaking Generational Chains (Ezekiel 18)

The challenges with family dynamics and past issues can be seen in the biblical concept of "iniquity." However, Ezekiel 18:20 declares that a child shall not bear the iniquity of the father. There is a struggle to break free from difficult situations and cycles. This is a story of a "dark night of the soul," where betrayal, systemic injustice, and personal heartbreak converged during a season of global isolation.

The world had shut its doors during the pandemic, but for me as a mother, the silence was deafening for a different reason. Separated from my children, I had sat in a darkness that wasn't just physical, but spiritual. The weight of the absence of my two daughters led me to a bottle, and the bottle led me to a night that changed everything: A DUI. Yet adding to my charges and giving my mother-in-law yet another reason to keep me even further away from my children. To the point I couldn't drop off birthday cakes or gifts at the door and resulted in her placing a restraining order to add to my destruction legally. For the simplicity of me needing a restraining order on her abusive son. Seeking safety and stability for my children as well as myself.

While I had drowned in my grief missing my daughters and having the ability to go to work and at least having a purpose in college, like "Pharaoh" was at work in my life. My mother-in-law, seeing my vulnerability, did not offer a hand to lift me up woman to woman mother to mother; instead, she used the law as a weapon. She seized the $54,000 insurance settlement check from my car accident from the insurance company and kept pandemic relief checks and tax return—papers like that of my W2s for 3 years, into her own hands. To keep me as a mother bound, the grandmother of my daughters and her son used the legal system as a cage, refusing to sign papers for a child that was not even his biologically, also he refused signing the divorce papers as I had a son in the mix of the pandemic by another man. Tried applying for food stamps and during the pandemic I had only qualified for $14 a month. It effectively was shackling me as a parent and a mother's ability to work or find peace. Because now having my mother-in-law file for child support also becomes a barrier to pay for children that me as their mother already paid for everything for sounds insane. While already getting pandemic checks and food stamps and DTA cash benefits worth thousands. For the children I had already paid for and raised working myself into severe exhaustion. In the period of the pandemic, she had collected thousands of dollars. And had even provided my husband and girlfriends with a free apartment. In which she had food, utilities, everything and more covered for them. Using the money she had scammed me and the system using her grandchildren. Though I had always known for a fact if she had been a grandmother in Dominican Republic and not having all the money the important and powerful people in office and the resources and the income plus the courts backing her she would have gave them children back right away immediately after finding out that I was finally out of the homelessness that her son put me and our daughters in.

In the midst of this financial and legal warfare, a darker rot was revealed. The family's history was marred by the very sins they accused me of. Shows how my mother-in-law and her actions as a mother, a grandmother, a woman, and a wife were always clearly way more questionable than anything I would ever have done even on a drunken moment. His mother years ago had slept with her best friend's husband and that is how she conceived her son meaning my husband. She ought to be ashamed of herself. As I struggled to reclaim my financial aid and my dignity, and a under the table stable job truth began to leak from the cracks: accusations of generational trauma and abuse within the family that spanned decades. I was the one being called a "sinner" by those hiding shadows much longer and darker than my own. Finding out that my husband had been sleeping with his friend's teenage daughter and her little best friend from school. I had also found out that my father-in-law had touched and sexually molested my sister-in-law. She had also later mentioned that my husband had also committed these same nasty disturbing acts to her children, his own nieces and nephews.

Biblical Parallels: Finding my own Story in the Word

My journey mirrors several figures in the Bible who faced false accusations, financial theft, and the "spirit of heaviness."

The Betrayal of Laban (Genesis 31)

Like my mother-in-law holding my tax papers and insurance money, along with my pandemic relief funds. Jacob's father-in-law, Laban, was a master of deception. He changed Jacob's wages ten times and held his family hostage through debt and contracts. But God spoke in Genesis 31:12: *"I have seen all that Laban has been doing to you."* God is the ultimate witness to stolen wages and diverted funds.

The False Accusations (The Story of Susanna)

In the biblical Apocrypha, Susanna was a virtuous woman falsely accused of "sleeping around" by elders who were themselves corrupt. She faced the death penalty based on their lies until the truth was revealed. My story echoes the "shaming" used to cover up the accuser's own family scandals. Proverbs 19:9 warn: *"A false witness will not go unpunished, and whoever pours out lies will perish."*

The Chains of Injustice (Isaiah 58:6)

The refusal of the son to sign legal papers to "keep me chained" is a form of spiritual and legal bondage. The Bible speaks directly to this in Isaiah 58:6: *"Is not this the kind of fasting I have chosen: to lose the chains of injustice and untie the cords of the yoke, to set the oppressed free and break every yoke?"*

Overcoming Adversity (Philippians 4:13)

Facing such overwhelming challenges can feel impossible, but the Bible offers a source of strength. Philippians 4:13 states: *"I can do all things through him who gives me strength."* This can serve as a reminder that even in the deepest struggles, there is a source of power to help you persevere.

The most jarring element of this history is the backdrop of faith. These individuals were devout yet presided over a home defined by abuse and hypocrisy. Their religion served as a thin veil for the monsters they harbored.

Looking back, at the level of hypocrisy is concerning. Yet also very impressive at the same time. It is a testament to the fact that monsters do not always hide in the dark; sometimes, they sit in the front pews, while the only person willing to act as a savior is the one the world has already written off.

A Journey Through Silence and Survival

Trauma, for many, is not a single event but a series of rooms one is forced to walk through. My journey began under the shadow of a profound violation of trust. The silence finally broke, leading to an abrupt departure and a vanishing from one life into the threshold of another. However, the escape from one nightmare only led us to a new one, more complex form of cruelty.

When we relocated, the sanctuary we hoped for was replaced by an environment of abuse and hypocrisy. The toxicity was so profound that one sibling, at a young age, chose the uncertainty of the streets over the "safety" of our home, forced to raise themselves and find a life among friends because the one provided by family was uninhabitable.

Inside that house, a cycle of betrayal resumed. In a house filled with adults, protection came from an unlikely source. Though this individual struggled with personal demons, they possessed a moral clarity that the "sober" adults lacked. Even in their darkest moments, they were the only ones who offered the only version of help they knew how to give.

I had childhood trauma since I was a child about getting either touched or molested while we lived in Puerto Rico by my father's wife's teenage son. Until one day he told his wife that he'd picked us up at school and took us out to get ice cream. We never looked back till this day, never heard from her or her family after so many years of just one day disappearing like that. Thought the beating and touching was done. After years of never seeing her son ever again. When my father's new girlfriend moved us out here after just meeting her at the beach in Puerto Rico. Just to move into Massachusetts and Her mother had been so mentally, physically, and verbally abusive with my twin sister and me. This caused my brother to run away from her home and practically stay with friends and learn to raise himself by that time he was about 10 or 11 years old. At the time our father was in jail for a shooting he committed at a local park. Her husband, which was my father's girlfriend's father, used to either touch or molest my twin sister and me. When she wasn't around the only one who defended us was her brother before he had passed away. Though her brother showed to have experienced inner issues with staying in church due to things like alcohol and drug addiction. He was clearly a good man and wasn't trying to touch molest or abuse nor physically abuse my twin sister and I in any way shape or form. If anything, even on his drunken drugged up days he helped us. My father's girlfriend's parents were full-blown Christian. The traumatizing kind that always felt the spirit hopped on one leg for more than half the service kind Christians even singed for the church they attended a Pentecostal church and identified as Bangelicos. The level of hypocrisy in people is either impressive or concerning.

As a young child practically being raised by the church and even spent so much time with nuns at their sanctuary home. I was filled with nothing but questions with two main questions in mind.

What are common responses to experiencing betrayal by trusted adults as a child, and how might these manifest in adulthood while seeking Christ with another perspective?

What are the psychological impacts of growing up in an abusive and hypocritical environment? Like that of the oppressive abusive from that of people of the church?

When a child is betrayed by trusted adults, especially in a home or church environment that is abusive or hypocritical—they often learn survival responses like people-pleasing, emotional numbness, hypervigilance, or deep distrust of authority. These patterns can follow them into adulthood, shaping how they seek Christ from a new perspective: they may fear being judged by God, struggle to trust spiritual leaders, or feel torn between longing for faith and remembering past harm. Growing up in an abusive or spiritually hypocritical environment can also create shame, confusion, fear of punishment, and difficulty forming healthy boundaries, because the people who claimed to represent God used their power in harmful ways. Yet many adults who come from these backgrounds develop strong discernment, a hunger for truth, and a more personal, authentic relationship with Christ, rebuilding their faith in a way that breaks old patterns rather than repeating them.

Biblical Perspectives on Hypocrisy and Abuse

The Bible does not ignore the reality of "monsters in the front pews" and offers stern warnings and deep comfort:

Judgment of Hypocrisy: Jesus famously condemned religious leaders who were outwardly righteous but inwardly "full of dead people's bones," calling them "whitewashed tombs" (**Matthew 23:27-28**).

Protection of Children: Scripture places an immense value on children, stating that anyone who causes a "little one" to stumble would be better off drowned in the sea (**Matthew 18:6**).

God's Compassion for the Broken: God is described as "close to the brokenhearted" and saving those who are "crushed in spirit" (**Psalm 34:18**).

Healing from Betrayal: The Bible acknowledges the pain of betrayal by those close to us. In **Psalm 55:12-14**, David laments that it was not an enemy but a "companion" and "close friend" who betrayed him

What gave me honors in my resilience, my heritage, and my spiritual restoration I have found within myself researching my Dominican Dominion as Resilience. It reframes my journey from a "victim of hypocrisy" to a "masterpiece of restoration."

The Altar of the Loom: A Restoration and Heritage

To look at a finished tapestry is to see order and beauty, but to look at the back is to see a chaotic tangle of knots and loose threads. My life was once that tangle—a series of "rooms", "led with the sting of violence, and the hollow echoes of religious hypocrisy. From the shores of the

Dominican Republic to the beach house of Puerto Rico, New York, and to the streets of Massachusetts and more, my story was one of enduring the unimaginable. Yet, through the teachings of leaders like Pastor Mike Todd and the ancestral wisdom of my heritage, I have learned that God is the Master Weaver. He does not discard the broken threads; He uses them to create a garment of praise.

The First Stitch: Weaving through the Wilderness

My journey toward healing began with a return to the tactile. In my Dominican heritage, the art of weaving and sewing is more than a chore; it is a "material genealogy." When I began knitting and weaving blankets, I was physically manifesting the truth of Psalm 139:13: *"For You formed my inmost being; You knit me together in my mother's womb."*

Every loop of yarn was a rejection of the lie that I was "not good enough." After years of being told by everyone and a system that I was disposable, the slow rhythm of the needles taught me patience. As I created sewn clothing and evening gowns, I recalled the "Cultivo de Vida"—the vibrant Dominican dresses that represent life and resilience. In Exodus 35:35, God fills the craftsman with wisdom to embroider and weave. Every gown I construct is a refusal to remain in the "spirit of despair," replacing it instead with a "garment of praise" (Isaiah 61:3). I am no longer the woman sleeping in a park; I am the daughter of a King, draping myself in the dignity I was always meant to wear.

The Sanctuary of the Soul: Meditation, Yoga, and the Word

The chaos of my past—the 80-hour work weeks, the physical assaults and sexual assaults and the betrayal by family and close friends, and the loss of my children to a system fueled by lie-required radical stillness. This is where yoga and meditation became my medicine. For a body that had been touched without consent and beaten without mercy, yoga was a way to reclaim my physical temple.

In the quiet, I practiced Psalm 46:10: *"Be still and know that I am God."* Meditation allowed me to "take every thought captive" (2 Corinthians 10:5), silencing the voices of my husband's mother and the judges who saw a "drunk Dominican" instead of a grieving mother. Through therapy and reading, I realized that my loyalty was not measured by how much abuse I could tolerate, but by how much truth I could uphold. Proverbs 11:14 remind me that "in an abundance of counselors there is safety." Therapy gave me the language to speak the truth that the Pentecostal "whitewashed tombs" of my childhood tried to bury.

The Canvas of Hope: Art and the Miracle of New Life

After nearly 3 years I had been separated from my husband and his family. During the pandemic court fights and isolation, I found out I was pregnant with my first son. Though for like 8 months I was unaware of his gender. When the world of Massachusetts doctors told me to abort my son, claiming he would be deformed, I retreated into the creative and the spiritual. I spent hours coloring, filling pages with vibrant hues as a form of "graphic prayer." As I colored, I meditated on the miracles of the Bible—how God brings life from dead places.

I immersed myself in trendy hair and makeup styles, not out of vanity, but as an act of radiance. My Dominican culture prizes self-presentation as a form of strength. Psalm 34:5 says, *"Those who look to Him are radiant; their faces are never covered with shame."* Every time I mastered a new style, I was washing off the shame of the jail cell and the homelessness. I was preparing for the new season.

The birth of my son—perfect, healthy, and my "first boy"—was the ultimate confirmation of Matthew 18:6. While the world tried to cause this "little one" to stumble before he was even born, God shielded him. Like the story of Moses' mother hiding him in a basket of bulrushes, I hid my son in a basket of prayer, sermons, and faith until it was safe for him to emerge.

The Tapestry of a Survivor

Today, I look at the licenses I earned, the citizenship I fought for, and the son I protected, and I see a miracle. My Dominican heritage gave me the hands to weave, and my faith gave me the heart to survive. The hypocrisy of those who sat in the front pews while abusing, using, or talking down on me no longer defines my view of the Creator.

I am a weaver of blankets, a designer of gowns, an amazing hair stylist and a student of the Word and world. My life is no longer a series of rooms I am forced to walk through; it is a sanctuary I am building with my own hands. As it says in Joel 2:25, *"I will restore to you the years that the swarming locust has eaten."* The locusts took my home, my job, and my reputation, but they could not take the thread of life that connects me to the father. I am weaving a new story now—one of gold, purple, and scarlet—a story where I am finally, truly, good enough.

To heal from childhood trauma is to rebuild a house that was once burned down, and for me, that restoration is being woven together with thread, prayer, and the vibrant colors of my Dominican heritage. This journey is a testament to the belief that beauty can be crafted from brokenness.

The Loom of Heritage: Weaving and Sewing

In Dominican culture, textile arts like handweaving, embroidery, and sewing are traditions passed through generations, serving as a "material genealogy" where hands perform the spiritual task of rendering memory material.

Knitting and Weaving Blankets: As I knit one stitch after another, I am mimicking the divine craftsmanship described in Psalm 139:13

"For You forced my inmost being You knit me together in my mother's womb". Each row of a blanket becomes a tangible prayer, a "fabric of my life" that God is weaving into a masterpiece.

Sewing Clothing and Evening Gowns: Making clothing, especially elegant gowns, is a transformative act. In Exodus 35:35

God fills craftsmen with wisdom to do "all manner of work," including that of the weaver and embroiderer. My Dominican roots shine here; the national dress, "Cultivo de Vida," uses vivid colors and intricate lace to tell a story of cultural identity and resilience. Creating a gown is like the spiritual renewal mentioned in Isaiah 61:3 exchanging the "spirit of despair" for a "garment of praise."

The Sanctuary of Stillness: Meditation, Yoga, and Reading

Healing requires a quiet space to reconnect with the body and spirit.

Meditating and Yoga: Meditation is a biblical practice of focusing the mind on God's promises.

Philippians 4:8 instructs us to think on whatever is true, noble, and pure. In the stillness of yoga or meditation, I am practicing

Psalm 46:10 "Be still and know that I am God." It is a way to quiet the "terror of night" that trauma often brings.

Reading and Therapy: Therapy provides a safe space to find words for pain that feels unspeakable. Reading the Bible and engaging in therapy fulfills

Proverbs 11:14 which notes that "in an abundance of counselors there is safety." By reading, I "took captive every thought" to make it obedient to the peace of Christ

2 Corinthians 10:5

THE ART OF TRANSFORMATION: COLORING, MAKEUP, AND HAIR

Coloring: Using "

Healing Bible Verses

" Coloring books allowed me to meditate on Scripture while engaging in art therapy. It is a form of worship where "each swipe of color pulls healing into my heart".

Trending Hair and Makeup: In the Dominican Republic, beauty and self-presentation—including elaborate hair and jewelry like Larimar—are significant cultural expressions. Mastering these trends is an act of reclaiming my image.

Psalm 34:5 says, *"Those who look to him are radiant; their faces are never covered with shame."* As I style my hair or apply makeup, I am not just following a trend; I am affirming that I am "fearfully and wonderfully made"

Psalm 139:14 My healing is not just a personal victory; it is a cultural and spiritual one. Like the "Dorcas clubs" where Caribbean women used textiles to share oral histories and build community, my crafts are a way of "bearing witness". I am moving from a "whitewashed tomb" of hypocrisy into a home built on the "unfailing love" mentioned earlier.

Lamentations 3:31-33 Through every stitch, every breath in yoga, and every verse read, I am proving that even when a "ruthless breath" is like a storm, God is a "shelter from the storm"

(Isaiah 25:4). I am weaving a new story, one where the trauma of the past is finally covered by the "garment of praise."

This is what connects the timeline of major American events from 2008 to the present to today with biblical themes of justice, leadership, and restoration. These were some of the events that began here in America after the birth of my first daughter.

The Unfolding Scroll: America, 2008–NOW

From the financial collapse of 2008 to the 250th anniversary of the nation today, America has traversed a period defined by deep fragmentation and the search for redemption. Viewed through the lens of Scripture, these events are not merely political or economic milestones; they mirror biblical patterns of judgment, wilderness, and the enduring hope for a "Jubilee" of restoration.

2008: The Collapse of False Foundations

The era began with the Great Recession of 2008, a financial crisis driven by subprime mortgages and unchecked corporate greed. This economic shaking mirrors the warning in Matthew 7:26-27 about the foolish man who built his house on sand. When the rain falls and the winds blew, the house fell because its foundation was unstable. The crisis revealed that a society built solely on the accumulation of wealth is fragile, echoing Proverbs 23:4-5, which warns that riches "sprout wings and fly like an eagle toward heaven."

Simultaneously, the election of the first African American president marked a shift in the nation's identity. While seen by many as a moment of hope, it also revealed deep fissures in the land. This duality reflects Ecclesiastes 3:1, "For everything there is a season," indicating that times of breaking down and building up often happen side by side.

2016–2021: A House Divided

As the decade progressed, political polarization intensified, culminating in the contentious elections of 2016 and the unrest of January 6, 2021. The deep division between "Red" and "Blue" America brings to life the words of Jesus in

Mark 3:25 *"If a house is divided against itself, that house cannot stand."*

The rise of "post-truth" politics and the spread of misinformation during these years parallel the biblical warnings against deception.

Isaiah 59:14

Describes a society where "justice is turned back, and righteousness stands far away; for truth has stumbled in the public squares." The chaos at the Capitol and the fraying of social bonds serve as a modern testament to the spiritual confusion that occurs when truth is subjective.

2020: Pestilence and the Cry for Justice

The year 2020 brought the COVID-19 pandemic, a global "pestilence" that halted the world. In Scripture, such pauses often serve as a divine wake-up call.

2 Chronicles 7:13-14 famously states that when God sends pestilence, the remedy is for the people to "humble themselves and pray and seek My faith." The pandemic stripped away the illusion of control, forcing a confrontation with mortality and the need for community.

Amid the silence of the lockdowns, the killing of George Floyd ignited a firestorm of protests, demanding racial justice. This cry from the streets echoes the prophet Amos: *"But let justice roll down like waters, and righteousness like an ever-flowing stream" Amos 5:24*

It was a reminder that peace cannot exist without justice, a core tenet of the biblical mandate to care for the oppressed Psalm 82:3

NOW: The Year of Jubilee and Reflection

Today America stands on the threshold of its Semi quincentennial (250th Anniversary). In the Bible, the 50th year was the Year of Jubilee (Leviticus 25:10), a time designated for liberty, the forgiveness of debts, and the return of lost property. While America is not ancient Israel, this 250th milestone (five Jubilees) offers a profound spiritual opportunity.

It is a moment to ask if the nation will continue in the cycle of division or embrace a true Jubilee of spirit—releasing the debts of past grievances and "proclaiming liberty throughout the land." Psalm 33:12 declares, *"Blessed is the nation whose God is the Lord."* This suggests that true greatness lies not in economic power or military might, but in a collective character defined by mercy, justice, and humility.

The journey from 2008 to TODAY has been a walk through the wilderness. Like the Israelites who faced trials to test their hearts (Deuteronomy 8:2), America has been tested by recession, disease, and division. Yet the biblical narrative always points toward hope for those who return to the path of righteousness. As the nation marks 250 years, the invitation remains: to build on the rock, to seek justice, and to heal the divided house.

TODAY the world is navigating a period of profound upheaval that many observers and theologians view as a direct manifestation of biblical prophecy. From the largest humanitarian crisis in recorded history to escalating conflicts in the Middle East and extreme environmental shifts, these events align with the "signs of the times" described in Scripture.

The Crisis in Sudan: Famine and Civil Strife

As of early today, the Sudanese Civil War is entering its fourth year, resulting in what the UN describes as the world's largest humanitarian crisis.

The Current Reality: Over 33.7 million people require aid, and nearly 12 million have been forcibly displaced. Famine conditions, first confirmed in 2024, are persisting today, with half of the population facing acute food insecurity.

Prophetic Connection: Jesus warned in Matthew 24:7 that "nation will rise against nation, and kingdom against kingdom. There will be famines and earthquakes in various places." Sudan's conflict, fueled by internal power struggles and ethnic violence, mirrors the "wars and rumors of wars" that characterize the "beginning of birth pains"

(Matthew 24:6-8). Furthermore, theologians often identify "ancient Ethiopia" (modern-day Sudan) as a key nation involved in end-times conflicts surrounding Israel.

Israel: The "Cup of Trembling"

The situation in Israel and the Palestinian territories remains a focal point of global tension as this year begins.

The Current Reality: Despite various ceasefire efforts, daily truce violations continue, and regional escalations involving Hezbollah in Lebanon and tensions with Iran remain high. In Gaza and the West Bank Millions remain in need of urgent humanitarian support.

Prophetic Connection: Many points to Zechariah 12:2-3

which describes Jerusalem as a "cup that sends all the surrounding people's reeling" and a "heavy stone for all nations". The persistent focus of the entire world on this specific region aligns with prophecies that Israel will be at the center of international concern in the "latter days".

Fires, Hurricanes, and the Groaning of Creation

The natural world has seen unprecedented volatility throughout 2025 and into the first days of 2026.

The Current Reality:

Wildfires: 2025 was marked by "all-season" wildfires, including the devastating Palisades and Eaton fires in Los Angeles in January 2025, which destroyed over 16,000 structures.

Hurricanes: The 2025 Atlantic season was record-breaking, with 80% of hurricanes reaching Category 4 or 5 intensity. Major storms like Hurricane Melissa severely impacted the Caribbean. Places like Dominican Republic, Puerto Rico, Haiti, Cuba and more were heavily impacted.

Prophetic Connection: Biblical prophecy frequently links environmental catastrophes to the end of the age. Luke 21:25

Speaks of "distress of nations with perplexity, the sea and the waves roaring." The increasing intensity and frequency of these disasters are often interpreted as the "groaning" of creation Romans 8:22

As it is near a period of divine renewal.

The Collective Message: Readiness and Hope

Scripture teaches that these cataclysmic events are not meant to induce panic, but to serve as a call to spiritual readiness.

Sovereignty in Chaos: Theologians emphasize that despite global instability, God remains sovereign over the nations (Daniel 4:34).

The Year 2026: As the world marks this year, many are looking at the biblical concept of "watching and praying" (Mark 13:33), recognizing that while the world may be bracing for further chaos, the "birth pains" are leading toward a promised restoration.

By linking these global crises—from the starving families in Sudan to the fires in California and the unrest in Jerusalem —to the specific warnings found in the Bible, a clear pattern emerges that many believe signals a critical turning point in human history.

Both the realities of the history of the past as well as my heritage with the connections of both my history and its prophetic connections had continued in my thoughts throughout the years. Rewriting my story into a formal book creates a powerful narrative of self-advocacy and divine intervention. My story serves as a testament to the importance of healthcare knowledge and the spiritual strength required to survive when the system fails you.

The Sentinel of My Own Life: Medical Advocacy and Survival

In the quiet, early hours of a morning that would nearly think to be my last, I awoke to a reality of excruciating, localized agony. My body was unsteady in contradictions: cold to the touch yet drenched in a drenching sweat that left my skin ghostly pale. Every movement was a battle against a crushing pressure in my upper right quadrant, a pain so profound that even the basic dignity of a shower was an unattainable luxury. This was not merely an illness; it was a total systemic failure.

As a Medical Assistant and a former CNA, my training began to scream in the back of my mind even as my body withered. When I finally forced myself to the hospital I was met with the first of many dismissals: I was told I was simply "passing stones." Despite a procedure to widen my ureter, the pain remained relentless, stabbing force that no amount of prescribed pain killers could touch. When the medical staff pivotally misdiagnosed me with appendicitis and prepared to remove an organ on my lower left quadrant, the "medical big words" I heard them whispering became a death knell. I knew, with the certainty of both my education and my intuition, that they were looking in the wrong place. While about to prepare to remove yet the wrong organ.

In an act of desperation, lucid defiance, I removed my own IV and catheter and ran to my car and I fled driving to yet another nearby local hospital. I drove myself to Furled by a survival instinct that defied my high fever and blurred vision. I collapsed at the intake desk, my last conscious act being the attempt to provide my name and date of birth.

The truth was far more lethal than "stones": I had gone into full-blown septic shock. My gallbladder had not just failed; it had erupted, sending toxins through my bloodstream in a wave of "nursing home toxins" that had nearly extinguished my life. I vanished into the shadows of the ICU for 19 days—a period that mirrors the biblical themes of waiting and testing before a miraculous return.

Waking up nearly three weeks later with no memory of my arrival was disorienting, yet it brought profound clarity. While I was worried about the logistical chaos of my towed car at the hospital parking lot and unpaid bills, a deeper fire had been lit. My healthcare knowledge had not just been a career; it had been my literal savior. This experience has transformed my life, my perspective on life, and my appreciation for life ensuring that the voices of suffering are never again silenced by a misdiagnosis. I learned to appreciate my knowledge in the hardest possible way: by using it to save my own life. While changing my view and perspective on it.

Biblical Reflections on My Survival

My story resonates with several powerful biblical themes regarding healing and the "inward parts" of the body:

The Seat of Life: In the Bible, the "inward parts"—the kidneys, liver, and gallbladder area—were considered the "seat of life" and the center of human emotion and soul (Psalm 73:21, Job 16:13). When my "gall" (bile) was poured out through my system, it was a literal and spiritual battle for my very soul.

The Power of Truth: Just as I had to advocate for the truth of my condition against the "blindness" of the doctors, Psalm 107:20 reminds us that God "sent out his word and healed them; he rescued them from the grave". My ability to see the truth of my own illness was a gift of discernment.

Restoration after the Pit: Being in the ICU for 19 days mirrors the many biblical figures who spent time in a "dark place" before a great restoration. Psalm 103:2-4 serves as a perfect prayer for my recovery: "He redeems me from death and crowns me with love and tender mercies".

Strength in Weakness: At my lowest point, unable to hold a cup of water, I was sustained by a strength not of my own. Isaiah 40:29 says, "He gives power to the weak and increases the strength of those who have no might".

TODAY, as I looked back on the moments that defined my survival, none are as haunting or as holy as the day the ocean tried to claim me. It was a day that stripped away every credential, every title, and every ounce of human strength I possessed, leaving me with nothing but the raw, unadulterated power of faith. When the boat began to take on water and eventually succumbed to the depths, I found myself suspended in the vast, indifferent blue of the Atlantic, a speck of life in a wilderness of salt and waves.

The sinking of a boat is not just a mechanical failure; it is a spiritual crisis. As the vessel disappeared beneath the surface, the silence that followed was deafening. I was miles from the shore, the water was cold, and I had no means to call for help. In the physical realm, my situation was a death sentence. But as my body began to tire and the weight of the ocean felt heavier with every passing second, Because I never learned to swim. I realized that while my voice could not reach the shore, my spirit could reach the Heavens.

This experience was a literal manifestation of Psalm 69:1-2: "Save me, O God, for the waters have come up to my neck. I sink in deep mire, where there is no foothold; I have come into deep waters, and the flood sweeps over me." I had no flare, no radio, and no strength left to tread water. I simply began to pray, a silent cry from the depths of a soul that had already survived abuse, sickness, and betrayal. I told the Lord that if my work on earth was not yet finished, He would have to be my life jacket. Begged to not take me until my children no longer needed me.

The appearance of the Marine Police was nothing short of a miracle. In the vastness of the ocean, finding a single person is like finding a needle in a haystack of moving glass. They arrived not because they heard a siren, but because they were led. Their arrival was the fulfillment of Psalm 107:28-30: "Then they cried out to the Lord in their trouble, and he brought them out of their distress. He stole the storm to a whisper; the waves of the sea were hushed... and he guided them to their desired haven."

When the officers pulled me from the water, I knew I wasn't just being saved from drowning; I was being preserved for a purpose. Just as I had survived a ruptured gallbladder and septic shock, I had now survived the "great deep". I realized that God often allows us to reach the point where we can no longer save ourselves so that we can finally see His hand at work.

Today, I carry the salt of that ocean in my memory as a reminder of God's sovereignty. I am a woman who has been pulled from the fire and the flood. My life is a living testimony that when you are down to nothing but your faith, you find that faith is the only thing that was ever truly required to keep you afloat.

book weaves together the harrowing reality of my persecution and the terror my family endured with the spiritual framework of biblical trials and divine protection. It frames my own personal journey as one of a "Living Martyr" who stood as a shield between the darkness and my children.

The Shield of the Innocent: A Narrative of Persecution and Divine Preservation

To understand the weight of my life today is to understand the cost of loyalty that was never earned and a debt that was never mine. For years, I lived as a woman persecuted—not for my own crimes, but for the shadows cast by a husband who had bartered my safety and the lives of our children to men who knew no mercy. I became a living target in a war I never declared, finding myself repeatedly in the crosshairs of those to whom my husband had "owned" money. Had owed Street favors or better yet owed some type of karma to. I have lost count of the many times, different places and the many people who shot at me with guns. While holding my very young daughters. They had broken into my apartment held guns on the kids' faces and scared those children to death.

The most visceral memory of this persecution is the weight of my babies in my arms while the air around us shattered with the sound of gunfire. There is a specific kind of terror that takes hold when you are running for your life, your heart hammering against the small, innocent chests of your children, knowing that the lead flying through the air is intended to erase your life and possibly the lives of your children too. In those moments, I felt like a modern embodiment of the flight into Egypt described in Matthew 2:13, where an innocent family had to flee under the cover of night to escape a tyrant's decree of death. Like Mary, I held the "promise" of the future in my hands while the forces of destruction closed in.

The persecution was not limited to the streets; it violated the sanctity of our home. On several occasions, the doors were kicked in—the wood splintering like bone—as men with cold eyes and heavy steel invaded our sanctuary. I can still see the glint of the barrels as they pointed guns at my children, and I demanding the whereabouts of a man who had abandoned his post as our protector. He really had the audacity to run without looking back to ensure the safety of his children and wife. To see a weapon leveled at a child is to see the face of pure evil. It is the "terror of the night" spoken of in Psalm 91:5, a moment where the natural world offers no protection, and I was again forced to rely entirely on the supernatural. With the weight and running while holding my almost 5yr old and my newborn in a car seat. As they had gotten older to still carried that weight after almost 8 years of persecution and getting shot at with my children at hand. The realistic fact of not having one bullet hitting any of us. It was the most supernatural of it all. Jesus, his father, and the holy spirit placed those hands in every persecution my children and I endured. Thank you, Jesus, his father and the Holy spirit. He made all of them bullets missed and passed us every time all those years. Each and every time somehow showed me the unsupernatural way the higher power had worked throughout my lifetime.

The Bible is not silent on this kind of targeted cruelty. In the book of Lamentations 5:11-12, we see the descriptions of women and children being persecuted and violated because of the failures of the men in leadership. My life became a literal fulfillment of Psalm 10:8-9, where the "wicked lie in wait in hidden places" to "murder the innocent" and "catch the helpless." I was the "helpless" caught in a net woven by my husband's choices.

However, the connection to the Bible does not end with the suffering; it culminates in the preservation. Every time a trigger was pulled and missed, every time a home invasion ended without the loss of a child's life, it was a manifestation of Isaiah 54:17: *"No weapon formed against you shall prosper."* The world sees a woman who was "lucky," but I know I am a woman who was "walled in." Like the wall of fire God promised to be around Jerusalem in Zechariah 2:5, I felt a hedge of protection that the "bad people" could sense but could not penetrate.

Looking back from the vantage point of today, I realize that my persecution served a purpose. It stripped away my reliance on man and forged a spirit that cannot be broken by any bullet or a blade. I have walked through the "valley of the shadow of death" (Psalm 23:4) not just once, but a hundred times, and I did not walk alone. I am a survivor who carried the weight of both my children through the fire, proving that the love of a mother, backed by the power of the Almighty, is the only shield that truly holds.

MY Deliverance in Loíza

The first real vacation of my adult life was supposed to be a celebration—my long-delayed exhale after years of financial struggle, pandemic exhaustion, and the quiet resentment of knowing that the tax refund I depended on had been withheld by my mother-in-law for over 3 years. When the money finally reached me, it felt like a door God had kept closed for a season and then opened in His own time. I booked a first-class ticket to Puerto Rico, imagining beaches, rest, and the feeling of reclaiming a piece of myself. I even paid for a friend to join me, believing loyalty would be returned with loyalty. That belief dissolved the moment she abandoned me on the island, after the lust of man, and leaving me alone in a place I had never been back to for over

20 years, carrying only my luggage and a prayer. Once again relying on nothing but higher power.

Puerto Rico greeted me with beauty, but also with a reality I had not expected. In Loíza, a town rich with culture and history, I found myself in the wrong place at the worst possible moment. A dispute erupted in a parking lot—loud voices, sudden chaos, and then the unmistakable sound of danger breaking open around me. Over 50 men in the projects shooting at each other. With no knowledge at that time, it was the time of disputes between two gangs in Puerto Rico at war. More I will not describe the violence in detail; I can say that I stood in the center of something no tourist should ever witness. In that moment, I remembered Psalm 23:4: *"Yea, though I walk through the valley of the shadow of death, I will fear no evil."* I repeated it like a heartbeat, believing that if God had brought me this far, He would not abandon me now.

As I ducked behind a car, an elderly woman—small, quick, and brave in a way that felt almost biblical—opened her door and motioned for me to run inside. She pointed towards the inside of her home directly behind her. Ducking even lower to the ground. I ran toward her door and dropped inside her living room floor. She lived in Loíza her whole life, and without hesitation she sheltered me. Inside her home, the world outside felt distant, muffled, unreal. The severe sounds of so many guns being shot at once. She gave me refuge, water, and told me to breathe, and reminded me that strangers can become angels when God appoints them. Her kindness was a shield I had not expected. As everyone around me was scattering to save their own lives.

The people I met in that neighborhood—men whose appearances might have intimidated me and anyone in sight on any other day—became my protectors. After a feud war many had walked in the home since many of them were her son, grandson and their friends from those projects. They were direct, street hardened, and unfiltered, but they were also human beings who saw someone in danger when they walked in and chose to help. They guided me through the back roads, of Loiza late at night in the darkness watched over me, protected me, fed me, sheltered me transported me to the airport, and made sure I reached the San Juan airport safely. Even directing me to the proper lanes and the people that will guide me to the proper plane flight I had been searching for. Their presence reminded me of Hebrews 13:2: *"Do not forget to show hospitality to strangers, for by so doing so have entertained angels unawares."* In my case, the angels looked nothing like the ones in paintings, but their actions spoke for them.

When I finally reached the airport, exhausted and shaken, I discovered that the friend I had paid for—my supposed companion—was already on the plane. She had security around her, using my past mistakes, my criminal record, and even my family history as justification for her "protection." It was surreal to see her sitting comfortably while I was questioned, watched, and treated as if I were a threat. Or a terrorist arriving on the plane. The irony was painful: I had survived real danger outside, only to be treated like a danger inside.

When I boarded the plane, she looked at me as though she had seen a ghost. Her eyes widened—not with guilt, but with the shock of someone who truly believed I would not make it back. That looked like everything had been said. It said she knew where she left me. It said she knew what could have happened. It said she never expected to see me alive.

The flight home was long, tense, and humiliating. I felt the weight of suspicion pressing on me from every direction. While the flight on air extended from a 3-hour flight to a 5-flight. Due to a storm in the cloud's midair. Yet even then, I remembered Joseph's words in Genesis 50:20: *"You meant evil against me, but God meant it for good."* What was intended to break me became a testimony. What was meant to isolate me revealed who I truly was—and who God had always been.

Puerto Rico was not the vacation I imagined. It was a trial, a revelation, and a deliverance. I left the island not with souvenirs, but with a deeper understanding of survival, faith, and the unpredictable ways God sends help. I learned that danger could come from the people I trust, and salvation can come from the people, I fear. I learned that sometimes the valley of the shadow of death is a parking lot in Loíza, and sometimes the rod and staff that comforted me were the hands of strangers who refuse to let me fall.

Most of all, I learned that my story—messy, complicated, and imperfect—is still being written. And this chapter, though born from fear, ends in gratitude. I walked into Puerto Rico seeking rest, but I walked out carrying a testimony.

Deliverance From a House Built on Sand

There are stories we inherit and stories we survive. Mine began in a marriage that looked stable from the outside but was built, as Jesus warned in Matthew 7:26, on sand—shifting, unstable, and destined to collapse under the weight of truth. My husband carried a lifetime of unresolved trauma, addiction, and generational dysfunction, and I carried the hope that love could fix what only God could heal. What followed was a journey through emotional, financial, and spiritual devastation that ultimately became my testimony of deliverance.

From the beginning, stability was a stranger in our home. My husband could not hold a job for longer than 50-60 days, drifting from one workplace to another, leaving behind excuses, anger, and unpaid bills. Each time he lost employment, the consequences fell on me. Each time he borrowed money from friends or family members. That also always fell on me. Each time he owed his drug dealers money. That also fell on me, including all the unpaid bills and having to buy food with no food stamp benefits. Since being legally married and sole provider making enough at the time I could not qualify for stamps. I worked long hours, often to exhaustion, trying to keep us afloat. Yet despite my efforts, we were evicted repeatedly, moving from apartment to apartment like wanderers without rest. His addictions—to drugs, to alcohol, to chaos—consumed every paycheck, every opportunity, every moment of peace.

His mother enabled him at every turn. As an only child, he had been raised without boundaries, accountability, or consequences. She defended him even when his behavior spiraled into dangerous territory, insisting he was misunderstood, insisting he was "a good boy at heart." But the truth was darker. His father had a history of violating boundaries in ways that harmed the family deeply, and those patterns echoed through the generations. The dysfunction he grew up with became the dysfunction he brought into our marriage.

As his addictions worsened, so did his behavior. He betrayed our marriage repeatedly, seeking validation in places that were not only inappropriate but deeply disturbing. I will not describe the details, but I learned that some of the people he pursued were far younger than any adult should ever be involved with. His mother dismissed it, just as she dismissed everything else, creating a cycle of denial that allowed harm to continue unchecked.

At home, the abuse took many forms. He stole my money, drained my accounts, and even took my car while I slept after long shifts. When his substance caused physical problems that affected our intimacy, like that of his masculinity, he blamed me, turning his shame into violence. When he desired to insert his penis in wrong places like that of my anus. He would also turn to violence. Telling me things like I wasn't woman enough to handle it. What he considered grown woman sex positions. That not only severely and deeply hurt me. But were also very uncomfortable and for me was also demining and humiliating as woman and mother. I lived in a constant state of fear of his anger, fear of his addictions, fear of what he might do next. Yet I stayed, believing I could fix him, believing that if I prayed hard enough, worked hard enough, loved hard enough, something would change.

It was then that I turned fully to Scripture. Psalm 34:18 says, *"The Lord is close to the brokenhearted and saves those who are crushed in spirit."* I clung to that promise. I realized that God was not asking me to endure suffering in silence. He was calling me to step out of bondage, just as He called the Israelites out of Egypt. My marriage had become a place of oppression, and leaving it was not an act of abandonment, it was an act of obedience.

Breaking away was not easy. Trauma does not release its grip quickly. But with every step I took toward freedom, I felt God strengthening me. I found support in unexpected places, courage I didn't know I had, and a sense of self that had been buried under years of chaos. I learned that survival is not just about escaping danger; it is about reclaiming identity, dignity, and purpose.

Today, I stand not as a victim but as a survivor. My story is not defined by the abuse I endured but by the strength it took to walk away. I am living proof of Isaiah 61:3—God's promise to give *"beauty for ashes, the oil of joy for mourning, and the garment of praise for the spirit of heaviness."* What was meant to break me became the foundation of my testimony.

I survived a marriage that was toxic in every sense of the word. I survived betrayal, addiction by others that broke a family that wasn't of my own, instability, and generational darkness. And through God's grace, I emerged not only alive but renewed. My past is no longer a prison; it is a testament. A reminder that even in the darkest and deepest. A light of hope can be found.

When Strength Is Not Enough—A Mother's Fight Through Darkness

There are seasons in life when even the strongest among us are brought to the edge of ourselves. I never imagined that I, a strong independent Black woman with an education, discipline, and a reputation for resilience, would one day be confined to a psychiatric ward. Yet that is where my journey led—not because I lacked strength, but because the weight placed on me became heavier than any human being should be expected to carry. My collapse was not a sign of weakness; it was the natural result of a system that failed me, a family that manipulated the truth, and a world that too often punishes mothers for surviving what others created.

My husband's mother had always enabled him. As her only son, he was treated like the golden calf of the household—untouchable, unquestionable, and worshipped in ways that blinded her to the destruction he caused. No matter how reckless or dangerous his behavior became, she defended him. She ignored his addictions, excused his irresponsibility, and dismissed the harm he brought into our children's lives. While she claimed to fear me enough to file a restraining order—one that prevented me from giving my own children birthday gifts, she allowed her son to drive intoxicated with them in the car in the middle of the night. She allowed him to involve them in violent situations no child should ever witness. Like that of him being involved in drive by a shooting with my young children seating in the back seat of the car. She normalized what should have been condemned.

Her influence extended far beyond her home. She had connections within the Department of Children and Families, and those connections shaped the narrative. Suddenly, my exhaustion from working multiple jobs became evidence of instability. My emotional distress became proof of unfitness. My attempts to protect my children became overreacting to aggressive anger. And when the pressure finally broke through my defenses—when the sleepless nights, the fear, the isolation, and the constant battles overwhelmed me—I was hospitalized. Not because I was dangerous, but because I was human. I had been crying in sorrow too loud for too long. And both his family and the system needed me both tamed and caged like an animal. While doctors felt having me medicated was necessary. An issue that extended even into the pandemic despite my pregnancy for my son. I had been placed on many medications from anti-depressants to anti-psychotic medications. It kept my mind at a slow pace that I was unable to control living in paranoia and chaos.

Inside the psychiatric ward, I felt stripped of everything—my identity, my motherhood, my voice. I was medicated, monitored, and isolated even more so still being persecuted by my husband and his friends and his 3 newfound bisexual girlfriends and some of his very impressive hypocritical members of his family, while pregnant for my son. While the woman who helped create the chaos outside used my absence to secure guardianship of my daughters. She collected state benefits worth thousands of dollars, while I, unemployed and fighting to rebuild my life, still found a way to celebrate my daughter's quinceañera. I braided both of my daughter's hair with products that cost nearly two hundred dollars per child, yet she could not offer even ten dollars for a simple jar of styling jam. Knowing that I was an unemployed mother on welfare. Her priorities were clear: to have full control, collect money from the state and local governments, and the appearance of being the savior in a story she helped destroy.

Through it all, I found myself returning to Scripture—not as a ritual, but as a lifeline. I thought of Job, a righteous man who lost everything not because he was flawed, but because he was targeted. Like Job, I found myself asking God why suffering had found me, why injustice seemed to triumph, why the wicked prospered while the innocent was silenced. Job 1:22 says, *"In all this, Job did not sin by charging God with wrongdoing."* I held onto that. I learned that questioning God is not the same as abandoning Him. Pain does not cancel faith; it reveals it.

I also remembered Hannah, a mother whose tears were misunderstood as madness. In 1 Samuel 1, Eli the priest thought she was drunk when she was praying from a place so deep that words failed her. I saw myself in her—misjudged, mislabeled, misunderstood. Yet God honored Hannah's cry, and I believed He would honor mine.

When I felt powerless, I remembered the story of Hagar, a woman cast out into the wilderness with her child. In Genesis 16, God met her in her lowest moment and revealed

Himself as *El Roi*— "the God who sees me." Even when the courts did not see me, even when the system did not see me, even when lies overshadowed truth, God saw me. He saw my motherhood, my sacrifices, my sleepless nights, my love. He saw the injustice. He saw the manipulation. He saw the truth behind every closed door.

And when I felt like the walls of the psychiatric ward were closing in, I remembered Paul and Silas in Acts 16— imprisoned not because they were guilty, but because they were inconvenient to those in power. And it might be a disturbance to those trying to seek power. They prayed and sang hymns in the darkness, and God shook the foundations of the prison. My walls did not crumble physically, but spiritually, something broke open. I realized that my confinement was not the end of my story; it was the beginning of my testimony.

Today, I stand as a mother who refuses to give up. I am still fighting for my children, still advocating for injustice, still proving that my love is stronger than any lie talked about me. I am the mother who, even with no job, found a way to celebrate milestones. I am the mother who showed up, even when injustice made her stay away by hundreds of feet and who sacrifices, who loves without limits. I am the mother who survived a system designed to break women like me. Strong independent educated women with more fight, loyalty, resilience, and with more pure honesty then many human beings can count. Yet became more solid in any relationship with friends or family members than any rock can withstand.

My story is not one of defeat. It is a testament—a declaration that even when the world tries to silence you, God still hears your voice. Even when people twist the truth, God still knows your heart. And even when you are pushed into darkness, God still provides a path back to the light.

My Constant reminder as a mother yet again

Even in my darkest moments, I held onto faith. I remembered Psalm 147:3: *"He heals the brokenhearted and binds up their wounds."* I remembered that God sees what people hide. I remembered that truth does not stay buried forever. My time in the psychiatric ward did not define me— it refined me. It forced me to confront my pain, reclaim my identity, and rebuild my strength from the inside out.

My story is not one of defeat. It is a testament—a declaration that even when the world tries to have silenced me, God still heard my voice. Even when people made up stories and lies over twisting the truth, God still knew my heart. And even when I was pushed into the pit of darkness, with feelings of loneliness and sorrow God still provided a path back to the light of many hopes as well as refined faith.

Survival, Accountability, and the Grace of God

There are moments in my life that split my story in two, the person I was before, and the person I became after. My DUI was one of those moments. It was a night that could have ended my life, the life of the person with me, and the lives of strangers on the road. It was a night defined by recklessness, fear, and consequences, but also by a miracle so profound that no police report, no courtroom, and no human explanation could ever fully capture it. The officers believed alcohol kept my body loose enough to survive the impact. But I know the truth: it was God, the Son, and the Holy Spirit who spared me. Somehow yet again.

The Night Everything Went Wrong

I decided that night that could have destroyed everything. I got behind the wheel intoxicated, a choice that was not just irresponsible, but dangerous. The speed, the chaos, the loss of control, it all happened so fast that it felt unreal, like watching someone else's life unravel from the outside. The person with me panicked and ran, only to be arrested moments later. I didn't know that he had been considered on the run from the halfway house. The feds had placed him. He had just been released then, because he had already been convicted and completed many years in federal prison. For a federal Rico charges for selling guns years ago. The situation escalated from reckless to catastrophic in seconds. Before I knew it my face my car and everything had already been all over the news and google search bar. For both my terrible accident and the scandal of criminal that had been arrested with me on the scene.

Cars were totaled. Metal twisted. Glass shattered. Sirens filled the air. And yet, somehow, I was still breathing. Somehow, I was still conscious. Somehow, I walked away from a scene that should have ended in tragedy. Yet the total amount of cars completely totaled due to my negligence had been over 10 cars.

The officers said it was the alcohol that saved me, that my body was too relaxed to tense up on impact. But I know better. I know that the only reason I am alive is because God placed His hand over me when I didn't deserve it. Though the air bags had also deployed it still hadn't touched me.

Arrest: Facing the Consequences

I was arrested on the scene. There was no escaping accountability, no talking my way out of the reality I had created. The flashing lights, the handcuffs, the cold air against my skin, it all felt like a harsh awakening. I had crossed a line that could not be undone.

But even at that moment, I felt something deeper than fear. I felt conviction. I felt the weight of my choices. And I felt God's presence, not in comfort, but in correction. The Bible says:

"For the Lord disciplines the one He loves."

— Hebrews 12:6

That night, I understood what discipline truly meant. Not punishment, but painful mercy. The chance to change before it was too late.

The Miracle: Why I'm Still Alive

When I replay that night in my mind, I don't see luck. I don't see coincidence. I see divine intervention. I see Psalm 91 in action:

"He will command His angels concerning you, to guard you in all your ways."

— Psalm 91:11

There is no earthly explanation for why I survived. The number of cars involved, the speed exceeded over 120 miles an hour, the impact, everything pointed toward death. And yet, God said "not today." He spared me not because I was righteous, but because He still had a purpose for me.

Sometimes God saves us from dangers we created ourselves. Sometimes His grace steps into the mess we made and pulls us out before we drown. That night was one of those moments.

The Aftermath: Shame, Reflection, and Transformation

Surviving was only the beginning. The real battle came afterward, facing myself. Facing the guilt. Facing the fear of what could have happened. Facing the reality that I had put lives at risk, including my own.

But in that darkness, God began to work on me. He didn't just save my life; He started reshaping it. He forced me to confront the parts of myself I had been avoiding, the pain, the recklessness, the lack of boundaries, the people I allowed into my life who were running from their own demons.

The Bible says:

"Be transformed by the renewing of your mind."

— Romans 12:2

That transformation didn't happen overnight. It came through tears, through prayer, through accountability, through learning to forgive myself while still owning the consequences.

A New Understanding of Grace

Grace is not pretty. It is not soft. It is not gentle. Sometimes grace looks like survival when you should have died. Sometimes grace looks like handcuffs that stopped you from destroying yourself. Sometimes grace looks like God saying, "I am not done with you yet."

My DUI was not just a mistake, it was a turning point. It was the moment God forced me to see the truth about my life, my choices, and the people I surrounded myself with. It was the moment He pulled me out of a path that would have ended in destruction.

Life Spared for a Purpose

I should not be alive. I should not be writing this. But God, in His mercy, intervened. He spared me not because I deserved it, but because He is a God of second chances. A God who rescues. A God who transforms. A God who uses even our worst moments to redirect our lives.

My DUI is not the end of my story, it is the beginning of a new one. A story rooted in accountability, humility, and faith. A story that reminds me every day that life is fragile, choices matter, and God's grace is real.

I am alive because God said so.

And now, I choose to live like it.

Survival, Courage, and the Miracle at the Park

There are moments in adolescence that carve themselves into memory so sharply that even years later, the emotions still echo. For me, one of those moments happened when I was a teenager, a moment that tested my strength, my instincts, and my ability to protect the person I loved most in the world. It was a moment that could have ended in tragedy, yet somehow, against every odd, it became a story of survival and an undeniable miracle.

Growing up, I was no stranger to being targeted. A group of kids at school, the same ones who taunted me, mocked me, and tried to intimidate me day after day, had made me their focus. Their bullying was constant, and although I learned to walk with my head high, the tension was always there, simmering beneath the surface. But nothing prepared me for the day everything escalated at the local park.

I was alone that afternoon, carrying my newborn baby brother in my arms. He was only weeks old, tiny, fragile, and completely dependent on me. I remember the warmth of his body against my chest, the way he slept peacefully, unaware of the world around him. I had gone to the park simply to get some fresh air, to clear my mind, and to give him a moment outside the walls of our home.

But the peace didn't last.

The same group that had bullied me for so long appeared, and before I could react, the situation spiraled. They surrounded me, too many faces, too many voices, too many bodies closing in. I felt the fear rise in my throat, not for myself, but for the tiny life I was holding. I was outnumbered, outmatched, and completely alone.

Yet something inside me shifted. Instinct took over, the instinct of a protector, a big sister, a guardian. I held my baby brother close, shielding him with my body as the chaos erupted around me. I moved with a kind of strength I didn't know I had, fighting not out of anger, but out of pure, desperate love. Every motion, every step, every breath was focused on one thing: keep him safe.

And somehow, impossibly, he stayed untouched.

Even as I struggled, even as I tried to defend myself, even as fear and adrenaline blurred the edges of the moment, my baby brother remained unharmed. Not a bruise. Not a scratch. Not a single mark on his tiny body. It was as if an invisible shield had wrapped around him, something stronger than me, stronger than the crowd, stronger than the danger.

Looking back, I know it was nothing short of a miracle.

When the chaos finally broke and the crowd scattered, I stood there trembling, exhausted, and shaken, but still standing. My brother slept in my arms, peaceful and untouched, as if the world had never erupted around us. I remember sinking onto a bench, tears burning my eyes, overwhelmed by the reality of what had just happened. I had been alone, outnumbered, and terrified, yet somehow, I had fought back. Somehow, I had protected him. Somehow, we survived.

That day taught me more about myself than any classroom, any textbook, or any adult ever could. It taught me that courage is not the absence of fear, it is the decision to act even when fear threatens to paralyze you. It taught me that strength does not always come from size or numbers, sometimes it comes from love, from instinct, from the fierce determination to protect someone who cannot protect themselves.

Most of all, it taught me that miracles do not always look like bright lights or dramatic rescues. Sometimes they look like a newborn baby sleeping safely in the middle of chaos. Sometimes they look like a teenage girl discovering her own resilience. Sometimes they look like survival when survival seemed impossible.

That day at the park was painful, frightening, and unfair, but it was also transformative. It showed me that even when I am alone, even when I am outnumbered, even when the world feels stacked against me, I am stronger than I think.

And it reminded me that protection can come from places we cannot see, in moments we least expect, in ways that defy explanation.

It was a moment that could have broken me.

Instead, it became the moment that proved I could not be broken.

Survival, Chaos, and the God Who Spared Me

There are seasons in life when survival becomes a full-time job, when every breath feels borrowed, every step feels risky, and every moment feels like a negotiation between danger and destiny. My short time living in Philadelphia was one of those seasons. I had gone there seeking safety, a fresh start, a place to breathe after running from situations that threatened my peace. Instead, I found myself in a neighborhood where chaos lived on every corner, where sirens were the soundtrack of the night, and where gunshots were as common as conversations.

Kensington Avenue was a world of its own, a place where addiction spilled into the streets, where people wandered like ghosts, where desperation hung in the air like humidity. Every day I felt like walking through a storm with no umbrella. I learned to duck without thinking, to scan every direction, to move quickly but quietly. I was almost seven months pregnant with my son, carrying life inside me while trying to protect myself. Every instinct in me was on high alert. My son's father was working in a pharmaceutical company at the time and those days I walked to the Bodega alone.

One afternoon, I walked to the Dominican bodega on Kensington Ave, a quick errand, nothing more. I remember the smell of fried food drifting from the kitchen, the familiar Spanish music playing behind the counter, the comfort of hearing my language in a place that felt so far from home. For a moment, I felt normal. Safe, even.

But safety in that neighborhood was always temporary.

As soon as I stepped out of the bodega, the world exploded into chaos. Shots rang out, sharp, sudden, too close. My body reacted before my mind could catch up. I dropped to the ground so fast that the impact sent a shock of pain through my belly. I remember clutching my stomach, terrified not just for myself but for the tiny life inside me. My heart pounded so hard I could hear it over the gunfire.

When the noise stopped, I pushed myself up slowly, my hands shaking, my breath uneven. And then I saw her, a young girl, no older than fifteen, lying still on the ground behind me. A child. Someone's daughter. Someone who should have been safe. The sight hit me like a wave of cold water. It was shocking. Heartbreaking. Mind-numbing. I didn't know her name, her story, or her dreams, but I knew she should have been alive.

And I knew that I could have been her.

The officers later said I was lucky. Neighbors said it was timing. Some said it was instinct. But I know the truth: it was God. It was the son. It was the Holy Spirit covering me and my unborn child in a moment when death was inches away. It wasn't the first time God spared me, and it wouldn't be the last.

I had left Massachusetts running from danger, desperate for safety, only to land in a place where chaos lived outside my door. But that moment on Kensington Ave became a declaration, a reminder that no matter where I ran, God's hand was still on me. He had protected me through storms I created and storms I walked into unknowingly. He had shielded my son before he ever took his first breath.

When I walked back home that day, my legs trembling, my belly still aching from the fall, I carried more than fear. I carried revelation. I carried gratitude. I carried the understanding that my life, and my son's life, had been spared again.

It was a moment that forced me to confront the fragility of life and the strength of God's protection. A moment that reminded me that survival is not luck; it is purpose. It is called. It is graceful.

Philadelphia taught me many things, how to move through chaos, how to trust my instincts, and how to protect my child before he was born. But the most important lesson was this:

God's mercy is not theoretical. It is real. It is active. It is the reason I am still here.

And every time I think back to that day, the gunshots, the fall, the young girl on the ground, the heartbeat inside me still strong, I remember that my story could have ended there. But it didn't. Because God wasn't finished with me. Because He wasn't finished with my son. Because even in the middle of chaos, His hand never left us.

Trauma, Grace, and the God Who Pulled Me Back into Life

Some stories are born from joy, but others are carved out of pain so deeply it leaves a permanent imprint on the soul. My story is one of those stories shaped by loss, trauma, and moments of darkness so heavy that I once believed the world would be better without me. But it is also a story of grace, of divine intervention, and of a God who refused to let go of me even when I had let go of myself. Today, I stand more grateful for my life than I ever imagined possible, not because it has been easy, but because I now understand how fiercely God fought for me to stay.

Childhood Shadows: The First Loss That Changed Everything

Growing up, I learned far too early that life can break in ways you never see coming. A close family friend, a woman I loved like an aunt, was one of the first people to teach me that. She was warm, funny, and full of life, the kind of adult who made children feel safe. And then, suddenly, she was gone.

Her death wasn't peaceful. It wasn't expected. It wasn't something a child could make sense of. She died by suicide, and the shock of it cracked something inside me. I didn't understand the depth of her pain, but I felt the weight of her absence. I felt the confusion, the fear, the silence that followed. It was the first time I realized that adults could break too, and that sometimes, they broke in ways that left no room for repair. At her wake and funeral, the marks on her neck haunted my mind for years. She had hung herself with a television cable wire. And the marks were heavy all over her neck. Yet, what had haunted me more than that, was that her husband, of many years who lived with her and shared a home and children with her had showed up to her wake with another woman like as if it was normal. Like we should all be greeting and grieving at the same time same time. Her young son who had found her hanging there was so hurt and confused I could not comfort him. He was way too young with way too many questions. Not even me as a teenager, who I thought I knew and understood adults more.

Nothing stayed with me more than the day I walked her son whom I considered a little cousin to the corner store to buy candy after his mother's funeral. He had been the one who found her, and the trauma weighed on him more than any of us could understand. My father handed me money for all the children, and I tried to make the moment feel normal, but everything changed as we crossed the street. I was slightly ahead of him, and when a car came speeding toward us, I turned back and saw him standing there with his hands

114

raised, as if someone were holding them. He later told me it was his mother guiding him across the street, and even though we had just buried her, he was certain she had been there with him. The image of him walking with his hands lifted, looking like he was holding an invisible hand, stayed in my mind for years. Whether it was grief, comfort, or something beyond understanding, that moment has never stopped haunting me.

A Second Tragedy: The Son Who Carried Her Pain

Years later, tragedy struck again. Her son, the same boy who had found her body, the same boy who had been forced to grow up in the shadow of a trauma no child should ever witness, took his own life at just nineteen years old. He was still a teenager, still a child in so many ways, still trying to navigate a world that had already taken too much from him.

Losing him felt like losing her all over again. It was a wound reopening, a reminder that trauma doesn't disappear just because time passes. It lingers. It echoes. It shapes the way you see the world and the way you see yourself.

His death planted a seed of fear in me, a fear that pain was inherited, that suffering was inevitable, that maybe some people were simply destined to break. At only 19 years old he had shot himself in the head. A thought that had always haunted me for years. Especially because I had just dropped him off at home that day. And though he had been talking about his mother and a dream he had about his mother the night before. He seemed fine as if he was going to see my little brothers hang out. But when I saw my little brother crying on the porch he told me what had happened and what he had just seen. My mind was blown, my heart sunk, and my body felt paralyzed.

My Own Darkness: When I Believed the Lie That the World Didn't Need Me

As I grew older, life didn't get easier. I faced my own storms, heartbreak, instability, trauma, and a sense of isolation that felt suffocating. I carried the weight of my past, the grief of those losses, and the pressure of trying to survive in a world that often felt indifferent to my pain.

There were moments when I felt like I was drowning in my own thoughts. Moments when I believed in the lie that the world would be better without me. Moments when I thought I was doing humanity a favor by disappearing. The same darkness that had swallowed the people I loved began whispering to me too.

But every time I reached that point, every time I felt myself slipping, something stopped me. Something I couldn't explain. Something that felt like a force stronger than my own despair.

God's Intervention: The Grace That Held Me When I Couldn't Hold Myself

I didn't understand it at the time, but now I know exactly what it was: God's grace.

The Bible says:

"The Lord is close to the brokenhearted and saves those who are crushed in spirit."

— Psalm 34:18

I was crushed in spirit. I was brokenhearted. And God came close.

In my darkest moments, I felt something, a presence, a pressure, a pull, that kept me from crossing a line I could never come back from. It felt like God tightening His grip on me, refusing to let me fall into the same darkness that had taken the people I loved.

It wasn't dramatic. It wasn't loud. It was subtle, steady, and unmistakably divine. It was as if God Himself was saying:

"Not you. Not today. I still have plans for you."

And He did.

The Turning Point: Choosing Life, Choosing Healing

Surviving those moments didn't magically fix everything. Healing took time. It took honesty. It took confronting the pain I had buried for years. It took learning that my worth wasn't defined by my trauma, my mistakes, or my darkest thoughts.

It took learning that God's grace wasn't just something I read about, it was something I had lived through.

The Bible says:

"My grace is sufficient for you, for my power is made perfect in weakness."

— 2 Corinthians 12:9

I used to hate my weakness. Now I understand that it was in my weakest moments that God showed His greatest strength.

Gratitude: The Life I Almost Lost but Now Cherish

Today, I am more grateful for my life way more than I have ever been. I am grateful for the breath in my lungs, the purpose in my steps, the future I once believed I didn't deserve. I am grateful for the people who love me, the opportunities ahead of me, and the God who refused to let me go.

I am grateful that I survived what others did not.

I am grateful that I broke the cycle.

I am grateful that I am still here.

My story is not one of perfection, it is one of grace. It is one of a God who stepped into my darkness and pulled me back into the light. It is one of survival, resilience, and a future I once thought I would never see.

And now, every day I live with the reminder that my life is not a mistake, it is a miracle.

A Friend Sent in Due Season

Life has a way of surprising us at the exact moment we feel forgotten. I had been carrying the weight of federal probation fees, unstable housing, and the emotional exhaustion of trying to rebuild my life from the ground up for like the hundredth time. I prayed for relief, for redirection, for something—anything—that would remind me that God still saw me and that he had not left me. What I did not expect was that the answer would come through an old friend who had just walked out of prison after nearly thirteen years behind bars.

When he returned home, he carried the kind of humility and clarity that only time and hardship can carve into a person. He had missed birthdays, funerals, holidays, and entire chapters of life. Yet he stepped back into the world with a quiet determination to do right, to rebuild, and to give back. I never imagined that it would be him, of all people God would use him to help me during the hardest and darkest times of my life. He had known me as a friend of the family since I was about 12 years old. And had completed jail time with my father and another time with my older brother. Had even at some point from jail as a teenager become a connection over the phone between my mother and me.

We reconnected almost by accident, but the timing was too perfect to be of any coincidence. I was struggling—financially, emotionally, spiritually. My probation fees were piling up, and the fear of falling behind weighed on me every single day. Housing felt like an impossible dream to reach. I was doing everything I could, but the math never added up.

Then he stepped in, not with judgment, not with pity, but with the kind of generosity that felt like divine intervention.

He helped me pay my federal probation fees—something I had been losing sleep over. He helped me secure an apartment through the developmental housing authorities, giving me the stability I had been praying for. He didn't have much himself, having just come home with nothing but determination and a second chance. Yet he gave freely, quietly, and without expecting anything in return. His help felt like the embodiment of Galatians 6:2: *"Carry each other's burdens, and in this way, you will fulfill the law of Christ."*

What struck me most was how God used someone society had written off—someone labeled, judged, and dismissed—to lift me up when I was sinking. It reminded me of 1 Samuel 16:7, where God tells Samuel that *"man looks at the outward appearance, but the Lord looks at the heart."* The world saw a man with a record. I saw a man transformed. God saw a vessel.

His support came at a time when I felt invisible. I had been fighting so many battles alone that I forgot what it felt like to be helped and guided completely and correctly. But God has a way of sending people in due season—people who show up not because they must, but because they are meant to. My friend became a living reminder that blessings don't always come wrapped in the packages we expect. Sometimes they come in the form of someone who has walked through fire and emerged with a heart softened, not hardened.

His journey and mine intersected at a moment when we both needed redemption in different ways. He needed spiritual survival. I needed a lifeline. Together, we found a kind of healing that only shared struggles can create. His help didn't just stabilize my life—it restored my faith in God's timing, in second chances, and in the unexpected ways grace shows up.

Today, when I looked around my apartment, the one he helped secure, I saw more than the walls and furniture. I saw a testimony. I see proof that God can use anyone, from any background, to deliver hope. I see the truth of Romans 8:28: *"And we know that all things work together for good to them that love God."* Even the things that break us. Even the things that imprison us. Even the things that nearly destroy us. Jesus, his father and the holy spirit are aways at work in our lives.

My friend walked out of prison after thirteen years, but he walked into my life as an answered prayer. His story is one of redemption. Mine is one of restoration. And together, they form a testament to the fact that God never forgets His children—even when we feel forgotten by the world.

When the Healer Becomes Another Wound

Some people enter our lives during seasons of deep vulnerability, and because we are hurting, we mistake their presence for healing. I once believed that a man who stepped into my life during one of my most fragile chapters was sent to help me rebuild. Instead, he became another wound—another lesson, another disappointment, another reminder that discernment is not optional when you are recovering from trauma.

I had already survived storms that would have broken many others. I was exhausted, spiritually bruised, and trying to recover from years of betrayal, instability, and emotional warfare. Financial instability, domestic violence and so much more. I did not need another trial. I did not need another person to heal from. Yet that is exactly what I received. Another human being that could not fully be trusted. With a criminal mind.

He came into my life with the appearance of support, compassion, and loyalty. He helped me in ways that felt meaningful at first, and for a moment, I believed God had finally sent someone to stand beside me. He had helped me stabilized financially, physically, mentally, and emotionally. But as time passed, the truth revealed itself: he was a pathological liar, a man whose stories shifted constantly, whose words were unreliable, and whose intentions were far from pure. Being caught committing too many shady acts. With the ability to sustain a lie for years if given the chance.

I later learned that my husband—the same man who had caused me so much pain—was the one who turned him in to the federal authorities' years prior. And that all those years he had spent in federal prison was because my husband turned out to be one of the informative in his indictment. The first time I had given my body to him. He had pulled out a phone in hopes of recording me. Though I stopped him from recording but continued. That revelation alone should have been a warning, but I was too emotionally vulnerable to see the danger. Instead, I found myself caught in the crossfire of a feud that had nothing to do with me. I began to feel like he was using me financially, emotionally, and psychologically and in other ways to get back at my husband. Because he had already told me about everything I had tolerated from my husband and now acting like I was unable to tolerate anything from him. But the truth was it had been more painful. His criminal mind and shady acts were just the kind of person he is. Yes, I had been the pawn of revenge against my husband. But I had also been someone who he can manipulate in order ways as well. Everything he had said to the actions he was showing. The way in which he moved never showed to be who he had said he is.

He lied about everything—from small details to life-changing events. He fabricated stories, manipulated emotions, and created chaos. My twin sister twice had over $900 stolen from her car, both times he was the only one who had access to it. Still, he denied it. Still, he twisted the truth. Still, he played the victim. Had slept with another women and for years claimed that he didn't because she had been infected with HIV AIDS. I had already known her through my older brother and the mother of his son. In hopes that would get me to believe him. Instead, I questioned him as a person much more. Because it is not hard for me to research that type of information. We live in an excitedly small town. The US Marshalls picked him up at my home and said he had been on the run for over 5 years. The day they took him I realized that yet again he is setting me back financially and still playing around with my rent money. Despite the many times I got tired of being the one telling him, I do not ever touch anything that isn't mine. Especially money to please return to me the same respect I give. Before I knew he was taking more than giving and taking back the little, he gave and I was back to feeling like a single parent home hand feeding common sense. While still being the main provider with or without a job. Before I knew it, he owed me thousands of dollars. A man with several side jobs as well as collecting cash welfare benefits unable to pay me back or help with the bills completely sounded it utterly insane yet again. An annoying disturbing act that he continues to do every month setting me back financially. Even using my rent money behind my back to gamble sports bets. An act that needed to be cut off immediately.

The more lies he told, the more I realized he was not a healer—he was another source of harm. He had come into my life during a fragile season, and instead of helping me rise, he added weight to the burdens I was already carrying. He set me back financially. He caused more chaos in my life with my husband, my children, my family, and the people willing to disturb my peace on behalf of my husband and his family. He created chaos in what I believed was my newfound sanctuary of peace in my home with my son.

The final blow in any type of relationship whether friends or even having a spouse to share my life with had come when I discovered that my husband had been secretly involved with my best friend, a woman I trusted completely and who relied on a wheelchair for mobility. I had learned how she had been doing more than drugs with my husband for over 10 years. That had cut so deeply it felt almost biblical—like Judas's kiss, a wound delivered by someone close enough to know exactly where to strike. In that moment, I understood that staying wasn't saving him; it was destroying me. It became painfully clear that she had been hiding far more than drug use, carrying secrets that had been kept for years, and I've always struggled to trust people who can hide such things for so long periods of time let alone for years. That kind of secrecy, especially from those who claim to care, is something I can never overlook again. Yet the new so-called healer in my life as he had been doing the same shady acts and sneaky behavior and me finding hurtful lies with that man and the same women I trusted. Knowing I had already forgiven her for doing the same thing other thoughts were morally acceptable like taking my kids behind my back from my mother-in-law or my husband and hiding it from me. To fulfill their own secret animosity. When there are all they have to used against you. The children are what they are going to use. It was a game that people played often, especially during the pandemic. He became the 2nd man in my life that she had involved herself in what she knew I had been trying to heal from. For over a year she helped him cover that lie and made me believe that he had been walking and sleeping in the streets. Because I had kicked him out of my home. At the same home he had been acting as if I no longer wanted to tolerate his shady acts. He bluntly told me he would make sure I was homeless too. Though he hadn't fully helped me with rent or other bills since the day he helped me with obtaining the first, last, and security to move in. Yet even when he spoke to friends living in Philadelphia he had acted as if my home was his and he had been doing me favor. Trying to take full control of my sanctuary home was something I was not willing to tolerate from him. Even at one point began to act as if it was normal to begin trap house activities with my little brothers in my home. I had been time, that I forced him to pay me back and get a place of his own. He was not about to start draining me physically and financially to then have the audacity to say he wasn't like me. He's damn right he wasn't anything like me I had finally understood that I had been too good to be true for too long. And most certainly to the wrong friends, family, and the wrong men in my life. That he didn't deserve anyone as loyal and as solid as a rock like me. The time to decrease his level of access to me, physically, emotionally, and financially had to be done immediately. By all means necessary I had gone through things in life, which anyone else would have folded. I was not about to go back to the amount of abuse and hypocritic and their acts to tolerate anyone in my life or trying to come into my life in any way. I had tolerated from any relationship to define my level love and loyalty to anyone that wasn't Jesus himself.

He drained my energy. He confused my spirit. He gave me more to heal from, not less. He carried a lie over year and half of sleeping in the home of the same handicapped women. He had already known about my trust issues, yet all he wanted to do was add to the many things I needed healing and delivering to. I felt that same loss of identity came back to me. Going to back to how much betrayal I can tolerate or forgive as my means of love and loyalty. It did matter what I said or how I said it even if I cried, he was bound to still get caught up with a lie or even standing on some shady and sneaky business.

And yet, in the middle of all this, he had also helped me in real ways. That contradiction became its own kind of torment.

How do I reconcile gratitude with his betrayal? How do I process kindness from someone who also caused me harm? How do I heal from someone who once felt like a blessing? And has now become yet another life lesson?

Reconciling gratitude with betrayal is one of the hardest emotional knots to untangle, because it forces you to hold two truths at once: someone can give you moments of kindness and still cause you deep harm. Processing that tension means allowing yourself to acknowledge the good without letting it erase the pain and recognizing that gratitude doesn't obligate you to stay loyal to someone who broke your trust. Healing from a person who once felt like a blessing often requires accepting that their role in your life has changed—that what once helped you grow eventually became a lesson you had to outgrow. In time, gratitude becomes part of your history, betrayal becomes part of your wisdom, and you learn to carry both without letting either define your worth or your future.

The Bible is full of stories of people who appeared helpful but carried hidden motives. In Judges 16, Samson trusted Delilah, believing her affection was genuine, only to discover she was aligned with those who wanted to destroy him. Like Samson, I ignored the warning signs because I wanted to believe in the goodness of someone who showed me attention during a vulnerable time. Like that of the first time I gave my body to him in a very vulnerable time. He had pulled out his phone to record me. That should have been my red flag to leave. Yet for some reason, I checked him for it and continued to stay.

I also thought of Judas, who walked with Jesus, ate with Him, and appeared loyal—yet betrayed Him with a kiss. Betrayal rarely comes from strangers; it comes from those close enough to touch you. That realization helped me understand why his lies cut so deeply. It had been revealing way too many lies and animosity involving him and my husband and too many members of his family. War for crimes both committed in the past that only one of them had been incarcerated for.

Then there was the story of the Israelites in the wilderness. They were tired, hungry, and desperate for relief, and in their desperation, they accepted things that were not good for them. They even longed to return to Egypt—the place of their bondage—because pain can distort your perception. I, too, accepted behavior I should have rejected, and even condemned simply because I was tired of fighting too many battles alone for too many years.

But the biblical parallel that resonated most was the story of Lot's wife. God was pulling her out of destruction, but she looked back—and in looking back, she lost herself. I realized that every time I gave this man another chance, every time I excused another lie, every time I ignored my intuition, or those red flags. I was looking back at something God was trying to pull me away from. The lies he held for 4 years claiming to be jumped by members of my husband's family. When reality was, he had been too close to them the whole time. Making pretend to be committing suicide the same way my husband used to do. That way, knowing my guilt being too great I would always stay. Because of the very fights involving my family he knew I hate those fights and would still cause them between us. One way or another I had been back to hand feeding common sense.

I also saw echoes of King Saul, a man anointed with potential but consumed by insecurity, jealousy, and deception. Saul's instability made him dangerous to those around him, especially David. My friend's instability, his lies, his manipulation, his emotional games—created the same kind of unpredictable danger. I cannot hold solid loyalty to another liar, deceiver, manipulator, cheater and had no issues with theft not even the mother of his son with me so I knew he did my sister wrong at heart as well. I had always felt it and refused to admit in my soul and in my heart.

And then there was Esau, who traded his birthright for a moment of comfort. I realized that in my loneliness, I had traded pieces of my peace for temporary companionship. But like Jacob, God was calling me to reclaim what I had lost. Because the chaos he had created in my life was not for the weak. Finding myself trying to heal from the past. While creating ways to heal from the present-day actions.

The Bible warns in Proverbs 26:11, *"As a dog return to its vomit, so fools repeat their folly."* It was harsh, but it was true. I kept returning to someone who had shown me repeatedly that he was not safe, not stable, and not sent by God for me or he would have never deceived me and disrespected me too many times. Net alone lied that many times or withstood them lies that long not to mention set me back financially and added so much to my burden it was unreal. Would not have done not even half of what had already been done or continue to do. Knowing that I had been in the process of a long spiritual healing after having gone through so much in life.

Yet even in this painful chapter, God was teaching me. He was sharpening my discernment. He was strengthening my boundaries. He reminded me that not everyone who entered my life is meant to stay. Some people are lessons, not lifetimes of filled blessings.

Today, I am healing—not because of him, but despite him. I am learning to trust myself again, to trust God again, and to recognize the difference between a helper and a hindrance. My story is not defined by the people who hurt me. It is defined by the strength it took to walk away.

This is another chapter in my testimony—another reminder that even when people fail me, God never does.

She Was Never a Friend, And I Finally See It Clearly

There are women who walk into your life pretending to be sisters, but their spirit exposes them long before their actions do. She was one of them. For years, I tried to convince myself she was genuine, that her connection to family meant she cared about me. But the truth was always there, hiding in plain sight.

She was never the kind of woman who would defend you in a room you weren't in. She was the kind who added wood to the fire, feeding the mouths of people who wanted to dishonor my name. She was the kind who smiled in my face while sharpening knives behind my back.

And the signs were always there.

She only reached out to me when she wanted something, not love, not friendship, not support, but information. She messaged me just to ask who the father of my son was and what his gender would be, as if my womb was gossip for her entertainment. Never a "How are you?" Never a "Do you need anything?" Only questions that fed her curiosity and her conversations with people who wished me harm.

And still, I stayed quiet. Still, I gave grace. Still, I watched.

Dismissed for People She Talked Bad About

What made it worse was how she dismissed me for the same people she constantly talked down on. She would run her mouth about them, then turn around and treat them like royalty while treating me like I was disposable.

That's when I learned something important:

A woman who speaks badly about everyone will eventually speak badly about you.

And she did. Every chance she got.

Using My Children During My Lowest Moments

During the darkest season of my mental instability, when I was fighting battles no one saw, she used my children as leverage. She weaponized innocence. She tried to turn my babies into tools for her secret animosity.

But even then, I never returned the favor. Because children are never to be used as pawns, not even against an enemy. That's the difference between her and me.

She Looked Down on Me, Yet She Looked Up to Me

For years she acted like she was above me, like she was wiser, stronger, more experienced. But her actions told the real story.

Because somehow, someway, she started. trying to become me.

She suddenly wanted to go to college, just like me. She wanted to get her license to carry, just like me. She started working nonstop, just like me. She started talking like she was teaching me something, when I had already walked that path long before her.

She hid her imitation behind arrogance, but imitation is still imitation.

You cannot look down on someone you are secretly trying to become.

She Never Lifted a Hand, Only Added to My Fall

When I was drowning, she didn't throw a rope. She threw stones.

She made sure to be part of every conversation that tried to destroy me and my children. She stood with the crowd instead of standing with the truth. And now that I am rising again, I can feel she only came back to check if I was still down, to see if the fall had finished me.

But God didn't let it.

She Was the Kind of Woman America Introduced Me To

She was the kind of woman I encountered too often in America:

- women who tear each other down
- women who compete instead of uplift
- women who lie to make themselves look better
- women who collect government money while flipping it in the streets
- women who date street men and think that gives them power

- women who confuse fear with respect

She built an indestructible persona out of chaos, drama, and survival of the wrong kind. But when it comes to being a woman, a mother, a wife, a sister, a friend, she could never compare to Carolina.

Because Carolina Is Built Different

There wasn't a single one of them working as much as me, going to school as much as me, enduring as much as me.

Because being Dominican, truly Dominican, means being forged in faith, resilience, and dominion.

It's not something I put on. It's something I *am*.

It's the fire in my blood from Quisqueya. It's the strength of my ancestors from the first island of the Americas. It's the spiritual authority God placed in me, here, in Puerto Rico, and everywhere my feet touch.

There could never be another me.

Because God didn't duplicate my purpose.

And That's Why She Could Never Break Me

She tried to slander me. She tried to isolate me. She tried to imitate me. She tried to monitor me. She tried to replace me.

But she could never be me.

Because what God put inside me is not something you can copy, steal, or fake.

It is dominion. It is calling. It is identity. It is Carolina.

And that will never change.

An Anti-So-Called History of the Black people of the past.

Its connections to the scattering while being justified using scripture and the very bible. While watching my deep bible stories, I had accustomed to during my own personal global isolation. I had come across a prophetic bible story. That had changed my perspective on not just the story of the black people regularly edited stories we learn in school. But another text that is older than what I could have ever imagined. It talked about everything that I had thought I knew. From the Pentecostal church I grew up going to go to since I was a child. Though the kind of Christians within my up bringing were more hypocritical than holy. I was ready to learn more about what I thought I had known. About the book of Revelation being wrong. That when Revelation Chapter 13 talked about the Beast, the Mark and the Persecution of the Saints it was not some far off event in the distant future. But is something that is going on right here right now and today and even in America. It talked about the people that were targeted. The people that were being marked and the very people who were being systematically oppressed by this very Beast system were the very descendants of the biblical Israelites themselves.

Like most, maybe it was a bit questionable to me, and I needed to continue to watch. Thought it could have been some type of conspiracy theory. Something that would make one ask questions. Like that onto why the church hadn't taught us the book of Revelation in this way. Why so many preachers have spent centuries pointing to Rome, Europe to some type of Anti-Christ of the future. But never once examined or researched what had been happening right here. To the specific group of people that match every single prophetic description in the scripture. Truth being a connection that is best to not be seen or known to those specific groups of people. The very system that failed my children and me. Are the very system that has worked overtime to hide this Revelation. My entire view of history and my view of these life events also changed as well as my view on the bible. Also, this made me change my whole understanding of the very people of God and who they were. It changed my perception of the economic system, the legal system, and the religious system. In which all of them were designed to target these specific groups of people. Something that made me understand not just the suffering of my ancestors; but also, my own suffering today. And even living in what he considered to country of opportunity in the US.

Revelation starting on chapter 13:1 "And it stood upon the sand of the sea, and I saw a Beast rise up and out of the sea. Having seven heads and ten horns. And upon his horns ten crowns and upon his heads the names of BLASPHEMY". Now right away I needed to understand what such a thing meant. I needed to understand what this Beast represents. In biblical prophecy Beast represents KINGDOMS, EMPIRES, AND POLITICAL SYSTEMS.

In Daniel, Chapter seven it had been made very clear. The four Beast in Daniel are four KINGDOMS. "So, When John sees this Beast rising up and out of the sea. He sees a governmental system. The power structure is rising. But here is what most preachers or teachers miss. That the sea of the biblical prophecy represents us the people. Multitudes as well as the Nations and tongues as mentioned earlier. When I mentioned the Diaspora and the scattering of people and nations. Revelation 17:17 tells us this in a very raw and in an explicit manner. "So, this Beast rises from among the nations. Specifically, from the gentile nations, the nations of the world. Yet, what does it do as verse 2 will tell us "And the Beast which I saw was like onto a Leopard, and his feet were as the feet of a bear. His mouth as the mouth of a lion, and the dragon gave him his power and his seat and gave him GREAT AUTHORITY. This is describing a composite empire. Taking characteristics from all the NATIONS from all the previous world EMPIRES. The lion is Babylon. The bear is Medio Persia, the leopard is Greece, and now we have Rome. We also have a continuation of Rome. In which is the Western European colonial system. That has dominated the entire world for the past 500 years. This is something that is not difficult for us to even really see if we paid closer attention. As we continue to study the word as well as its prophetic Bible stories. Learning ways to connect them with our history and our heritage to help heal from the inner most ancient stories of humanity where it all began.

As we continue the dragon in which is Satan according to Revelation 12:9 gives this Beast system. Its power we are talking about a satanically empowered governmental system. That, as mentioned earlier, has the characteristics of all previous empires. Now what happens next? Verse 3 "And I saw one of his heads as it were wounded to death and his deadly wound has healed, and all the world wondered after the Beast. Thinking about this Roman Empire, the Roman Empire felt correct. And had received a deadly wound. But the question is. Did it really die. Or did it just transform? Was it not able to continue through its mission or what's known in the bible as prophecies. Through the holy Roman Empire and through the papal system through colonialism. Through the same British empire mentioned previously. And now through the American Hegemony. The Beast system never died. It transformed and changed its name.

It just changed forms and the whole world and every nation on earth. Operates under this Western dominated system. They wonder after it, they worship it, they follow its economic models. Its political structures and its cultural values. Verse 4 will mention this. "And they worship the dragon, which gave them power unto the Beast. And they worship the Beast saying, who is like unto us the Beast. Who can make war with him. When we look around us, not just for centuries, even today.

What system dominates the entire planet?

Understanding what system dominates the entire planet requires looking at how countries, economies, and cultures are connected, and most scholars agree that the world is shaped by a global capitalist system that influences nearly every aspect of life. This system organizes nations into powerful "core" countries that control wealth and resources, "semi-periphery" countries that are developing but still dependent, and "periphery" countries that are often exploited for labor, raw materials, and cheap production. It affects everything from international trade and migration to political decisions, cultural trends, and the daily cost of living. Institutions like the IMF, World Bank, and global trade agreements operate within this same structure, reinforcing the flow of power and money toward wealthier nations. Because of this, the global capitalist system doesn't just shape economies—it shapes identities, opportunities, and the way entire regions, including the Caribbean and the Dominican Republic, fit into the world. Now that is what I call an Anti-Perfect So-Called History.

What culture is exported to every corner of the globe?

American popular culture is the most widely exported culture in the world, spreading to nearly every corner of the globe through entertainment, technology, and consumer trends. Hollywood movies, pop music, fast-food chains, global fashion brands, and major tech companies all carry American values, aesthetics, and lifestyles far beyond the United States. Digital platforms like social media and streaming services amplify this influence even more, making

American slang, music, celebrities, and trends instantly recognizable worldwide. This cultural reach—often called "soft power"—shapes global tastes, behaviors, and even aspirations, making American culture one of the most dominant and far-reaching cultural forces on the planet.

WHO's military power is so powerful? That no nation dares to challenge it not even to joke about challenging it, like that of the warnings of my father.

The nation our God the father warned us about is the United States, whose military power is so extensive that most countries avoid even the idea of challenging it. With the world's largest defense budget, advanced technology, global intelligence networks, and a vast system of military bases, the U.S. can project force almost anywhere on the planet. Its navy, air power, and nuclear capabilities create an unspoken understanding in international politics: direct confrontation with the United States is something nations approach with extreme caution. This dominance shapes global alliances, conflicts, and diplomacy, and it explains why even my father with his limited English spoke of it with such seriousness—because in the modern world, few forces influence global behavior as strongly as American military power.

Whose economic system, capitalism, free markets, central banking controls the wealth of every nation?

The economic system that shapes the wealth of nearly every nation is the global capitalist system, built on free markets, international trade, and central banking networks that connect countries into one interdependent financial structure. No single person or secret group controls it; instead, it operates through powerful institutions such as national central banks, the International Monetary Fund, the World Bank, and global financial markets that influence currency values, interest rates, and investment flows. Wealthier nations—especially those with strong currencies, advanced industries, and major financial centers—hold more influence within this system, which is why decisions made in places like the United States, the European Union, and major Asian economies can affect the entire world. This system doesn't control nations in the sense of ownership, but it does shape their economic options, their vulnerabilities, and the way money moves across the planet.

This is the Beast, and this is the system, and it's whether people like me take the time to realize it or not. They do worship it and everything that comes with it. They also serve it as well as dependent on it. Such a subject is only personal as it connects to our past and present, but also our future. As cited on Verse 7 "It was given unto him to make war with the saints and to overcome them. And power was given to him over and all kindreds. Like that of the tongues and nations mentioned earlier. The Beast makes war with the saints. Not with sinners and not with the pagans with the saints and with god's people.

The people that in the bible god talks about them being the chosen people, the covenant people, and the people of the promise lands that is now a reflection on the fact that if this Beast system is making war against a specific type of people. And the systematic warfare against this we would see the patterns of oppression, of targeting, and of attempts to destroy their identity, their culture and their existence.

Economic Mark Revelation 13:16-17 "And he Caused all small and great rich and poor free and bond. To receive a mark in their right hand or in their foreheads and that no man might buy or sell. Save onto him that had the mark or the name of the beast or the number of his name.

For centuries prophecy teachers had speculated about microchips, bar codes, digital currencies, and of course that of today and its technology like that of AI is in fact playing a huge role in the final implementation.

What if this mark is not just about future technology?

What if this mark was really about identity? Being branded by the system about being forced to operate. Within an economic structure that controls whether you can participate in commerce or not. Thinking about the Redlining like that used by politicians during campaigns. This is the very systematic structure where entire communities were marked on Maps with red lines. These communities had been denied access to loans for home mortgages and to business capital. They could not buy property. And not participate in selling property. They could not participate in the economic system on equal footing. These people were predominantly the descendants of slavery and predominately those identified as African American or Black today as well as the Hispanics.

If we look at the number, the wealth gap in America is not accidental. Studies have shown that the median wealth of families of the African descendants or black population is roughly one tenth of that of family of European descent or white population.

How does one tenth of an entire population happen in the land of opportunity?

A question like that carries a lot of weight, because it's really asking how a country built on the idea of opportunity can still produce such deep inequality. When one-tenth of a population struggles—whether through poverty, homelessness, incarceration, or lack of access to basic resources—it doesn't happen because people failed individually. It happens because systems shape outcomes long before personal choices ever enter the picture.

In the United States, a mix of historical forces and modern structures creates these gaps. Generations of unequal access to education, housing, healthcare, and stable wages leave entire communities starting from behind. Economic shifts—like the decline of manufacturing, rising living costs, and stagnant wages—hit certain groups harder than others. Immigration patterns, racial discrimination, and regional disparities also play a role, creating pockets of opportunity and pockets of hardship within the same nation. Even though the U.S. is known as the "land of opportunity," opportunity is not evenly distributed; it depends heavily on where someone is born, what resources their family has, and how society treats their identity. One of the hardest challenges I too had been facing.

So, when one-tenth of a population struggles in a country that promises possibility, it's not a contradiction—it's a sign that the promise is real for some, but not yet accessible to all. An act of opportunity that had many communities as well as society as a whole to have raised many questions.

How does an entire geography remain economically suppressed Generation after Generation?

An entire geography can remain economically suppressed for generations not because the people lack talent or will, but because systems, history, and power structures lock whole regions into disadvantages long before any individual is born. When a place stays poor across centuries, it's almost always the result of forces far bigger than personal effort.

An entire region can remain economically suppressed for generations when historical wounds—such as colonization, slavery, resource extraction, or political instability—create long-lasting structures that limit opportunity from the start. Once a place is positioned as a source of cheap labor, raw materials, or strategic control, powerful nations and global markets often reinforce that role, making it difficult for the region to build independent wealth. Weak infrastructure, underfunded schools, limited access to capital, and cycles of debt keep communities from advancing, while outside investors and global institutions frequently extract more value than they return. Over time, these patterns become self-repeating poverty restricts education, limited education restricts income, and low income restricts political power, allowing the cycle to continue. This is how entire geographies—whether in the Caribbean, Latin America, Africa, or parts of the United States—can remain trapped in economic suppression long after the original cause has passed, because the systems built around them were never designed for their prosperity.

This is because of the systemic mark and the systemic barrier preventing full economic participation. Like that of banking discrimination. Not only is it documented and proven in court cases. That lending discrimination is based on race. Higher interest rates for the same credit scores. The denial of business loans at disproportionate rates. The inability to build generational wealth. This is because the same system itself is rigged to do exactly that prevent it. The prison of industrial complexes like that of mass incarceration has removed millions of people. Disproportionately from one demographic from economic participation entirely. Being unable to buy or sell being locked in a cage. You can't build a business with a felony record that has also kept you from employment. And if you do it would take decades longer than that of what an average white person will achieve.

This sounds like that of what Revelation 13 describes. A system that can control who can buy and sell. A system that marks certain people for economic exclusion. The mark is the identity imposed by the system as what had happened to me. The mark is the second-class status. The mark is that barrier that is placed on your identity so that you cannot thrive and be successful economically. It gets worse because we investigate legal persecution. Revelation chapter 13:7 says. That the Beast makes war with the saints and overcomes them. War in the modern world is not always military bombing. At times war can be and is legislative and sometimes can and is also judicial. Same way in the way I had been bonded after my trials and tribulations and all the people who contributed. Sometimes war is a systematic targeting through the laws designed to incarcerate to oppress the same way I have been living for years. This is not just to oppress but to also control. When we think about the 13th amendment, this is the amendment that "DIQUE "supposedly abolish slavery. Back in 1865 only that neither slavery nor involuntary servitude except as a punishment for crime. This is where all the parties involved should have been duly convicted as I was. Shall exist within the United States. This is when we pay attention to the DIASPORA mentioned earlier.

After slavery had ended, a series of laws that were called black code were enacted across the south. These were the laws that criminalized certain behaviors only accepted, maybe by freed slaves. The laws of vagrancy against being unemployed and even walking at night. This also included gatherings in groups. Whether it was a church service, a baptism, or a baby shower, or wedding. Suddenly thousands of newly freed slaves were arrested. For crimes that didn't exist prior, and once they had been convicted, they were released back to the plantations, to mimes, and factories as convict labor. Same convict labor I had to enact for my 4 years of federal probation. Same system being used today; slavery never ended it just changed and became legal under a much different name. An act used against blacks and Hispanics for generations. The blacks and Caribbeans as well as Hispanics began their journey being sent here to work. Now being treated with the same brutality to be deported for doing the same overworking their fingers to the bone.

As we fast forward to today like that of the war on drugs started centuries ago to have been designed to target these specific communities. As advisor President Nixon once said where he had admitted in a 1994 interview. That the war on drugs had been used to criminalize and disrupt communities. He stated that "we could arrest their leaders, raid their homes and break up their meetings and vilify them night after night on the evening news. They had lied about the drugs, and the mandatory minimum sentences the three strikes laws. The policies that had sent people to prison. For decades for non-violent offenses and most of the people who still fill prison even today. Are the people of African American or black people as well as the Hispanic descendants. Blacks make up about 13% of the US population. But nearly 40% of that population is the prison population. That's what it was like what I went through that had not been random nor coincidence. That is the systematic warfare through the legal system that is exactly as it had been revealed in revelation 13 prophesied. While we see the statistics and policies, we see the pattern. We see it still being repeated decades after decades and century after century. This is one of the targeted wars that have been happening. While still going on today.

As the spiritual and cultural dimensions. The mark on your forehead would represent your mind and your thoughts as well as your identity. While your hands represent the actions as well as your labor and deeds. In which would make this mark not just economical and legal; but also, psychological and cultural. Is the forced identity imposed by that very Beast system. This had been done to replace our true heritance.

Why is it that the descendant of the Israelites called African American? Why not Hebrew American? Why not an Israelite American?

The reason people in the United States with African ancestry are called African American rather than Hebrew American or Israelite American is because the term reflects the historical reality of the trans-Atlantic slave trade, not ancient lineage. Enslaved Africans were taken from many different regions, cultures, and ethnic groups across West and Central Africa, and because their specific identities were erased through slavery, the term African American became a way to acknowledge both their African origins and their American nationality. Labels like Hebrew American or Israelite American are not used because they describe religious or ancestral identities rather than the shared historical experience that shaped Black communities in the United States. Over time, African American became the widely accepted cultural and ethnic term, emphasizing heritage, history, and the struggle for civil rights rather than ancient descent.

In the Dominican Republic, the question of identity is just as complex, shaped by colonization, the trans-Atlantic slave trade, and centuries of cultural blending. Just as African Americans were given a broad label that erased their specific ancestral nations, Dominicans of African descent were also separated from their original ethnic identities and folded into categories like "indio," "moreno," or "mulato," terms created during Spanish colonial rule to distance the population from Blackness. These labels were not reflections of true heritage but tools of social hierarchy, designed to hide African roots and elevate European identity. As a result, many Dominicans grew up disconnected from the specific cultures, languages, and histories of the African peoples they descended from. The same forces that shaped the term African American—forced migration, cultural erasure, and the rewriting of identity by those in power—also shaped Dominican identity, leaving generations to rediscover their roots and reclaim the fullness of who they are beyond the labels imposed on them.

This is because with the new identity given by the system it removed them from their biblical lineage.

When talking about the slave trade, names and languages were changed and were forbidden. While their cultural practices were beating out of people. Families were torn apart so that knowledge could not be passed down. While we can see that this is not physical enslavement. This was a spiritual and cultural genocide. This goal was meant to take away memory, history, and to take away the connections of that very covenant that acts like a scroll directly at the middle of my Dominican flag. Something that had worked for many centuries while prophecy said this would happen. Deuteronomy 28: The curses for disobedience predicted everything. From ships to slavery. While serving other gods and losing their identity. Every single course was fulfilled.

The deleterious part is the revelation 13 is the religious deception of revelations 13. This was when it talked about withholding another Beast. That is coming up and out of the earth. With two heads and two horns. Like a lamb and with the Spake as a dragon. This is the false prophet. This is the religious power that looks like Christ and speaks like Christ. Like that of the church with slavery. Using the Bible to justify their darkest behaviors. Yet speaks the words of Satan and what religion has done. The very faith that should have liberated god's people had been weaponized to enslave them. Preacher coted Ephesians verse 5 servants be obedient to them that are your masters according to the flesh with fear and trembling they had used the bible to justify chains. They had used scripture to justify even rape. As mentioned earlier the bible has been used to justify people's darkest behavior specially of the most powerful as well as their allies. Using the bible and its scriptures were not just used to justify slavery and rape but also murder and the darkest brutality on humanity. They had taught us a Christianity that only teaches us submission to oppression. Instead of deliverance from it, this religious deception continues today. Something that has continued even today in so many churches that teaches that much prosperity without justice. And that heaven without addressing hell on earth and forgiveness without confronting the system. They are the ones that need to be held accountable. While the Vatican itself was complicit. Pope

Nicolas the 5h had issued a papal bull in 1452. It was called Dum Diversus and had giving Portugal the right to enslave Africans. This had been done perpetually as the church blessed the slave trade and profited from it. While the monasteries owned plantations the bishops owned the slaves. That Beast system had used religion to sanctify its evil. That false prophet that religious structure that looks holy yet serves the dragon that's still somehow happening today.

Following the bloodline and the prophecy that had followed us from ancient Israel to those same conditions we see today. This is not speculation; this is documented in history and in our DNA. Of the people who had been scattered and persecuted and marked as the bible had talked about. The 12 tribes chosen by the most high to be a light to the nations to carry his law and demonstrate his glory. When they disobeyed and broke that covenant Deuteronomy chapter 28:15 says that Moses had prophesied both blessings for obedience and curses for the disobedience.

Finding our inner calling as a Christian is not a gentle revelation. It is not a soft whisper floating down from heaven wrapped in pastel colors and easy answers. It is a soul-level upheaval, a holy disruption that shakes the foundations of who you think you are so God can reveal who you truly are.

It begins quietly, almost imperceptibly, a tug in your chest, a restlessness that sits behind your ribs like a stone you can't swallow. You try to ignore it, distract yourself, drown it in routine, but it keeps resurfacing. It presses against you from the inside, insisting that something in your life is misaligned. This is the first sign of a calling: God disturbing your comfort. Making one reevaluate their peace and tranquility as well as their level of wisdom and understanding.

Scripture rarely shows God calling people in peaceful moments. Moses wasn't meditating by a river; he was hiding from his past, dusty and exhausted in the desert. Gideon wasn't leading armies; he was crouched in fear, threshing wheat in secret. Paul wasn't seeking truth; he was blinded by his own certainty until God literally knocked him off his path.

God does not wait for you to be ready.

He interrupts you.

And when He does, it feels like being pulled into a wilderness, not a physical one, but an internal one. A place where the noise of your life fades and you're left alone with the parts of yourself you've been avoiding. Your fears. Your pride. Your wounds. Your excuses. Your false identities. God brings them to the surface not to shame you, but to strip away everything that cannot carry the weight of your calling.

This is the graphic part, not in a bodily sense, but in a spiritual one.

It feels like exposure.

It feels like being peeled open.

It feels like God placing His hand on the deepest parts of you and saying, "This must go."

Isaiah described it as being "undone."

And that is exactly what it feels like.

But in that undoing, something else begins to emerge as desire. Not the shallow kind that flickers and fades, but the deep, bone-level longing that feels like it was woven into you before you were born. Christians are often taught to distrust desire, but God uses it. He plants holy desires that refuse to die, no matter how many times you try to bury them under practicality or fear.

These desires feel ancient.

They feel like they are the truth.

They feel like home.

They pull you toward something you can't fully articulate, a direction, a purpose, a work that feels both terrifying and right. This is God speaking through your design.

And then there are your wounds. The places where life cut you open, where you bled emotionally or spiritually, where you thought you were broken beyond repair. These wounds are not detours from your calling; they are clues. God repurposes pain with surgical precision. The very places where you suffer become the places where you carry authority, compassion, and testimony.

Your calling often grows out of the soil of your suffering.

But God does not hand you the full blueprint. He gives you a fragment, a whisper, a nudge, a single step. And then He watches. Not because He is testing you like a teacher waiting for you to fail, but because calling requires trust. It requires obedience in the small before responsibility in the large. It requires surrender, not strategy.

You take one step.

Then another.

Then another.

And slowly, almost imperceptibly, something begins to shift. Your mind begins to transform its way of thinking. You start to feel alignment, not comfort, but clarity. A sense that your actions, your gifts, your desires, and God's voice are no longer pulling in different directions. It feels like your soul is finally exhaling after years of holding its breath.

This is the fruit of calling.

Not applause.

Not ease.

But alignment.

And when you reach that place, when you finally stop running, stop negotiating, stop pretending you don't feel the pull, you realize something profound:

Your call was never hiding from you.

You were hiding from it.

God had been whispering it all along, waiting for the moment when you would stop clinging to the life you built and open your hands to the life He designed.

Finding your calling as a Christian is not about discovering something new.

It is about surrendering to something God has been shaping in you for years. This happens long before we are even born.

It is the moment you say, with trembling honesty:

"Okay, Lord. I'm ready to become who You made me to be."

Dominican Dominion: A Raw, Vivid, Soul-Level on Power, Identity, and Biblical Calling

Dominican Dominion is not a political slogan, a tourist phrase, or a patriotic chant. It is something older, deeper, and far more visceral, a spiritual posture woven into the bones of the Dominican people, shaped by centuries of survival, resistance, and rebirth. It is the fierce, unbreakable sense of authority, identity, and purpose that rises from an island carved by colonization, faith, and the relentless will to endure.

To understand Dominican Dominion, you must feel the island's history under your skin, the Taíno earth, the African drum, the Spanish cross, all colliding, clashing, and ultimately fusing into a people who learned to stand tall even when the world tried to bend them. Dominion, in the biblical sense, is not domination. It is stewardship, authority, responsibility, and identity, the mandate God gave humanity in Genesis to rule with purpose, not cruelty. He had given us work. Before companionships or alliances, the very day he created humanity. And the Dominican story is soaked in that tension: the struggle to claim authority without becoming the oppressor, the fight to rise without forgetting the wounds that shaped the rise.

Dominican Dominion is the island's spiritual inheritance, the echo of Genesis 1:26-28 pulsing through a nation that has been broken, rebuilt, and reborn more times than history bothers to count. It is the belief, conscious or not, that God placed something fierce and unshakeable inside his people, something that refuses to die even when everything around them collapses.

The Roots: Dominion in the Bible and the Island's Soul

Biblically, dominion is the first gift, and the first responsibility God gave humanity.

"Let them have dominion...", not to exploit, but to steward, to shape, to protect.

Dominion is identity. Dominion is purpose. Dominion is calling.

But dominion is also dangerous.

When twisted, it becomes oppression.

When misunderstood, it becomes pride.

When forgotten, it becomes slavery.

The Dominican Republic has lived all three.

The Taíno people once held dominion over the land, not through force, but through harmony. Their dominion was gentle, rhythmic, rooted in the soil and the seasons. Then came colonization, and dominion was stolen, twisted into conquest. Africans were dragged into the island's story, carrying with them a spiritual dominion that no chain could break, a dominion of rhythm, resilience, and uncrushable identity.

Dominican Dominion was born in that collision:

the Taíno's harmony,

the African's endurance,

the Spaniard's religion,

all pressed together under the weight of history.

Dominion Through Survival: The Island That Refused to Die

Dominican Dominion is the spiritual muscle memory of a people who have been conquered, erased, enslaved, liberated, invaded, divided, and reborn. It is the instinct to rise, repeatedly, even when rising seems impossible. Before we were created or born it wasn't on us it was already in us.

It is the echo of biblical dominion expressed through survival.

Dominion in the Bible is not passive. It is active, gritty, embodied. It is the call to shape the world rather than be shaped by it. And that is exactly what the Dominican people have done for centuries.

They shaped culture out of trauma.

They shaped music out of pain.

They shaped identity out of fragmentation.

They shaped joy out of sorrow.

This is dominion in its rawest form, not power over others, but power over despair. I had been educating myself to do exactly that. Teach myself everything I hadn't been taught in any textbook I had ever read.

Dominion Through Faith: Christianity as a Forge

Christianity in the Dominican Republic is not a quiet religion. It is loud, embodied, emotional, and deeply woven into daily life. Churches are not just buildings; they are spiritual battlegrounds where people wrestle with God, with life, with themselves.

This is where Dominican Dominion connects most intensely to the Bible.

Dominion in Scripture is tied to image-bearing, the idea that humans reflect God's authority, creativity, and purpose.

Dominicans reflect this in their faith:

- in the way they pray with their whole bodies,

- in the way they worship with rhythm and fire,

- in the way they cling to God through storms, poverty, and uncertainty,

- in the way they believe in miracles because survival itself has been a miracle.

Dominican Dominion is the belief, spoken or unspoken, that God has placed something powerful inside his people, something that cannot be colonized, enslaved, or erased.

Dominion as Identity: People Who Carry Fire

Dominican Dominion is not political.

It is not nationalistic.

It is spiritual.

It is the fire in the Dominican voice, the rhythm in the Dominican step, the pride in the Dominican heart. It is the sense that no matter how small the island is on a map, its presence in the world is enormous, culturally, spiritually, musically, emotionally.

Dominican Dominion is the biblical mandate to rule, not with tyranny, but with creativity, resilience, and soul.

It is the belief that God gave this people a unique blend of strength and softness, joy and sorrow, rhythm and reverence.

It is the calling to rise, to create, to endure, to influence, to shine.

Dominica Dominion as Calling

In the Bible, dominion is a calling, a purpose placed on humanity from the beginning.

Dominican Dominion is that calling expressed through a nation's story.

It is the belief that:

- God placed authority in this people,

- God placed resilience in this people,

- God placed creativity in this people,

- God placed spiritual fire in this people.

Dominican Dominion is the island's way of living out Genesis, not perfectly, not painlessly, but powerfully.

It is the story of a person who learned to carry dominion not as conquest, but as identity.

Dominican Women and Dominion: A Raw, Vivid Power of Survival, and Biblical Identity

Dominican dominion is often spoken about as a national spirit, a fierce, unbreakable force that pulses through the island's history. But if you look closely, if you peel back the layers of politics, culture, and myth, you'll find that the truest carriers of that dominion have always been the women. Dominican women have held the island together in ways that history books rarely acknowledge. Their dominion is not loud or ceremonial. It is lived. It is embodied. It is carved into their backs, their hands, their prayers, and their endurance, their fight and their resilience.

To understand Dominican dominion through the eyes of women, you must understand what dominion means in the Bible. Dominion is not domination. It is authority, such as stewardship, identity, and calling. As we mentioned earlier, yet we still need its connection to women as well. It is the mandate God gave humanity in Genesis, not to crush, but to cultivate; not to rule over people, but to rule over chaos. And Dominican women have been doing exactly that for centuries: ruling over chaos, shaping life out of disorder, creating stability out of instability, and carrying a spiritual authority that no colonizer, dictator, or system could erase. Unaware is exactly what I had been doing for years living in America.

Back Then: Dominion Born in the Shadows

Dominican women did not inherit dominion through privilege. They forged it in the shadows.

During colonization, Taíno women were the first to carry the island's original dominion, a dominion rooted in harmony with the land, in community, in spiritual intuition. Their leadership was subtle but powerful. They were healers, cultivators, storytellers, and protectors. Their dominion was relational, not hierarchical.

Then came the brutality of colonization and slavery. African women were dragged into the island's story, but they brought with them a dominion that no chain could break, a dominion of rhythm, resilience, and spiritual fire. They carried culture on their hips, in their drums, in their lullabies whispered to children born into bondage. They carried faith in their bones, even when the world tried to crush it out of them.

Dominican women in this era lived dominion through:

- survival

- motherhood under impossible conditions

- spiritual resistance

- cultural preservation

- emotional endurance

Their dominion was not recognized, but it was real. It was the dominion of women who kept families alive when men were taken, killed, or silenced. Or even worse when the man in their lives failed at being providers or protectors. In the same way both men in my life had failed at their leadership. It was the dominion of women who prayed when praying was forbidden, who sang when singing was dangerous, who loved when love was a rebellion.

This is biblical dominion in its rawest form, the dominion of women like Deborah, who led a nation; Esther, who saved her people; Hagar, who survived abandonment; Mary, who carried the future inside her body.

Dominican women lived these stories without ever reading them. A part learned about our Anti-So Called-History that must be shared with the world in a full text form.

The 20th Century: Dominion in the Face of Dictatorship

Under Trujillo, Dominican women were expected to be silent, obedient, ornamental. But dominion does not die under oppression, it intensifies. The Mirabal Sisters, Patria, Minerva, and María Teresa, embodied a dominion that was both spiritual and political. Their courage was not just resistance; it was stewardship of justice, protection of the vulnerable, and obedience to a moral calling higher than fear.

Their dominion was biblical in nature, the dominion of women who stand in the gap, who confront evil, who refuse to bow.

Dominican women in this era carried dominion through:

- education

- activism

- secret organizing

- raising children in a climate of fear

- holding families together through scarcity

Their dominion was not celebrated then. But it shaped the nation.

Today: Dominion Reborn in New Forms

Dominican women today carry dominion in ways that are both ancient and modern. They are entrepreneurs, pastors, artists, mothers, students, activists, and leaders. They navigate a world that still tries to limit them, but they move with a spiritual authority inherited from generations of women who refused to break.

Their dominion shows up in:

- the way they pray with fire

- the way they hustle with determination

- the way they protect their families

- the way they build community

- the way they speak truth even when it costs them

Dominican women today are reclaiming dominion not as domination, but as identity, the identity God gave them before culture tried to define them.

The Biblical Connection: Dominion as a Woman's Calling

The Bible is full of women who carried dominion in ways that mirror Dominican women's history:

- Deborah led a nation with wisdom and courage.

- Esther used her position to save her people.

- Ruth rebuilt her life through loyalty and resilience.

- Mary Magdalene was the first to proclaim the resurrection.

- The Proverbs 31 woman ruled her household, her business, and her community with strength and dignity.

Dominion in Scripture is not masculine. It is human.

And Dominican women have been living that truth for centuries.

Dominican dominion, when expressed through women, becomes:

- nurturing without being weak

- strong without being harsh

- spiritual without being passive

- resilient without being hardened

It becomes the dominion of women who know who they are, who they belong to, and what they were created to carry.

Dominican Women as the Island's True Dominion-Bearers

Dominican dominion is not a theory. It is a lived reality, and Dominican women are its fiercest carriers. Another anti-perfect so-called history that many still do not address today. They embody the biblical mandate to cultivate, protect, create, and rise. They carry the island's history in their blood and its future in their hands.

Their dominion is not loud, but it is unshakeable.

Not violent, but powerful.

Not imposed but inherited.

Not forced but chosen.

Dominican women have always carried dominion, in the fields, in the kitchens, in the streets, in the churches, in the classrooms, in the boardrooms, in the quiet corners where survival is negotiated and identity is forged.

They are the living intersection of Dominican history and biblical calling.

They are the island's backbone, its heartbeat, its fire.

They are dominion in human form.

After Reading the book "I Never Thought I'd See the Day! by Dr. David Jeremiah"

In I Never Thought I'd See the Day! Dr. David Jeremiah presents a sobering examination of the dramatic cultural and spiritual shifts occurring in contemporary society. Writing from a Christian worldview, Jeremiah argues that the moral and ethical foundations that once shaped Western civilization are rapidly eroding. Through ten thematic chapters, he explores changes that previous generations would have considered unimaginable, using Scripture, historical reflection, and cultural analysis to illustrate how these developments align with biblical warnings about spiritual decline. The book functions not only as a critique of modern culture but also as a call for renewed faithfulness among Christians navigating an increasingly complex world. This is what had originally inspired me to write this book.

One of Jeremiah's central concerns is the widespread abandonment of biblical values. He describes a society that has redefined morality, normalized behaviors once considered harmful, and embraced a worldview centered on personal autonomy rather than divine authority. This shift, he argues, mirrors the prophetic warnings found in passages such as 2 Timothy 3, which describes a future generation characterized by self-centeredness, moral confusion, and hostility toward truth. Jeremiah suggests that the cultural landscape of the twenty-first century reflects these biblical predictions with unsettling accuracy.

Another major theme in the book is the diminishing influence of the Christian church. Jeremiah contends that many churches have compromised their doctrinal foundations to remain culturally relevant. He critiques the rise of entertainment-driven worship, diluted preaching, and the reluctance to address controversial moral issues. According to Jeremiah, this spiritual softening has weakened the church's ability to serve as a moral compass. Instead of shaping culture, the church is increasingly shaped by culture. This reversal, he argues, leaves believers spiritually vulnerable and contributes to the broader moral decline.

Jeremiah also highlights the growing disregard for Scripture. He notes that the Bible is often dismissed, reinterpreted to fit personal preferences, or replaced entirely by subjective opinion. This trend stands in stark contrast to biblical commands to guard sound doctrine and remain anchored in truth. Jeremiah connects this erosion of biblical authority to the broader cultural shift toward relativism, where objective truth is replaced by individual interpretation. He warns that without Scripture as a foundation; society loses its moral and spiritual bearings.

A significant portion of the book addresses the rising hostility toward Christianity in public life. Jeremiah observes that Christian beliefs are increasingly portrayed as outdated, intolerant, or irrelevant. He compares this cultural climate to the early church, which faced persecution for refusing to conform to societal norms. Drawing on Jesus' warnings that His followers would face opposition; Jeremiah encourages believers to remain steadfast despite cultural pressure. He frames this hostility as part of a larger spiritual battle described in Ephesians 6, emphasizing the need for spiritual vigilance.

Despite the book's heavy themes, Jeremiah does not write from a place of despair. Instead, he offers a message of hope and resilience. He urges Christians to respond to cultural decline not with fear, but with courage, conviction, and compassion. He emphasizes the importance of prayer, Scripture, community, and personal integrity. Jeremiah reminds readers that throughout history, God has sustained His people through times of moral confusion and societal upheaval. The final chapters of the book focus on God's sovereignty, reassuring believers that no cultural shift can undermine God's ultimate plan.

Ultimately, I Never Thought I'd See the Day! serves as both a warning and a call to action. Jeremiah challenges readers to recognize the spiritual significance of contemporary cultural changes and to live with renewed purpose in response. The book argues that while society may be drifting away from biblical truth, Christians are called to stand firm, shine light in dark places, and embody the hope of the gospel. Through its blend of cultural critique and spiritual encouragement, Jeremiah's work invites readers to reflect deeply on their role in a rapidly changing world and to recommit themselves to a life of faithfulness.

When I read Christianity in Latin America and the Caribbean, I see more than a history book—I see the spiritual map of my people. The chapter on the Dominican Republic feels like someone finally naming what has always lived beneath our skin: that our island was shaped not only by colonization and struggle, but by a faith that became woven into our identity long before we had the language to describe it. The author shows how Catholicism arrived with the Spanish, but it didn't stay as a distant institution; it sank into the daily lives of ordinary Dominicans—into our prayers, our celebrations, our sense of family, and even our understanding of suffering and survival. What moved me most is how the book explains that Dominican Christianity was never just about church hierarchy or doctrine. It was about the people—our ancestors—who carried faith through trauma, blended it with their own traditions, and turned it into something uniquely ours. Reading it feels like tracing the spiritual inheritance of the island, seeing how God, history, and identity have always been intertwined in the Dominican story.

Modern Pastors, Performance Preaching, and Biblical Standards

In today's religious landscape, a troubling trend has emerged: pastors who treat the pulpit as a stage, the sanctuary as a runway, and the gospel as a performance. Instead of humility, reverence, and biblical teaching, many modern preachers rely on theatrics, designer clothing, shock value, and emotional manipulation to attract attention. This shift reflects a deeper spiritual crisis, one that mirrors the warnings found throughout Scripture about false teachers, corrupted worship, and the danger of turning God's house into a spectacle.

One of the most visible expressions of this trend is the rise of pastors who preach in extravagant outfits, dresses, and that of male pastors wearing women high heels, luxury brands, and designer accessories, not as expressions of identity or culture, but as performative tools meant to draw attention to themselves rather than to Christ. Clothing itself is not the issue; But to me it is after a male pastor is preaching in women dresses and high heals. Scripture does not condemn fashion or self-expression. Yet the number of preachers dressed like women and coming down and across the room from the ceiling is beyond questionable. The problem arises when pastors use their appearance as a spiritual credential, implying that they have expensive attire. Like that of Chistian Dior is proof of divine favor or evidence that they "walk with Christ." This mindset directly contradicts biblical teaching. Jesus Himself warned against religious leaders who "love to be seen by others" and who "wear long robes" to gain honor (Matthew 23:5–7). The issue is not the robe, it is the motivation behind it.

This problem becomes even more disturbing when pastors incorporate sexualized movements, provocative gestures, or explicit metaphors into their sermons. Some modern preachers have been recorded humping the floor, thrusting into the air, or using graphic language to describe "impregnating the church with the Word of God." These actions are not creative illustrations; they are distortions of sacred truth. They turn the pulpit into a comedy skit, the sermon into a performance, and the congregation into an audience. Scripture is clear that the preaching of God's Word must be done with reverence, sobriety, and self-control. Paul instructs Timothy that pastors must be "temperate, respectable, self-controlled, and able to teach" (1 Timothy 3:2). Nothing about thrusting on the floor or mimicking sexual acts aligns with biblical standards of pastoral conduct.

Furthermore, the metaphor of "impregnating the church" is not only inappropriate but theologically inaccurate. In Scripture, the church is described as the Bride of Christ, not the bride of the pastor. Christ alone is the one who gives life to the church through His Word and Spirit. When a pastor positions himself as the one who "impregnates" the congregation, he symbolically replaces Christ with himself, a form of spiritual arrogance that borders on idolatry. Paul warns against this in 2 Corinthians 11:2–4, where he expresses fear that believers might be led astray by teachers who preach "another Jesus" or elevate themselves above Christ.

The use of expensive clothing as a spiritual symbol is equally problematic. Some pastors flaunt luxury brands, designer shoes, and high-priced accessories as evidence of

God's blessing. They preach prosperity through appearance, implying that material wealth is proof of spiritual authority. Yet Jesus taught the opposite. He warned that "life does not consist in the abundance of possessions" (Luke 12:15) and that leaders must not be "lovers of money" (1 Timothy 3:3). When pastors use wealth as a sermon illustration or as a badge of holiness, they distort the gospel into a performance of status.

This trend reflects a deeper issue: the transformation of the church into a spectacle. Instead of being a place of worship, repentance, and spiritual growth, many churches have become platforms for entertainment. Pastors act like influencers, comedians, or motivational speakers rather than shepherds. Their sermons rely on shock value, theatrics, and emotional manipulation rather than Scripture. This is precisely what Paul warned about when he wrote that a time would come when people "will not endure sound doctrine but will gather teachers who tell them what their itching ears want to hear" (2 Timothy 4:3). The modern church, in many cases, has become a fulfillment of this prophecy.

The mockery of Christ's church is not always loud or intentional. Sometimes it is subtle, a shift in focus from God to the pastor, from Scripture to performance, from holiness to entertainment. But whether subtle or blatant, it is dangerous. Jesus overturned the tables of those who turned the temple into a marketplace, declaring, "My house shall be called a house of prayer" (Matthew 21:13). Today, many pastors have turned the sanctuary into a stage, the sermon into a show, and the gospel into a brand.

The rise of performance-driven pastors, those who preach in extravagant outfits, use sexualized gestures, flaunt wealth, or distort Scripture for entertainment, represents a serious departure from biblical teaching. The issue is not clothing, creativity, or culture; it is motivation, reverence, and truth. Pastors are called to shepherd, not perform; to teach, not entertain; to exalt Christ, not themselves. When the pulpit becomes a stage and the pastor becomes the star, the church loses its purpose. Scripture calls believers to discernment, humility, and holiness, qualities that must be restored if the church is to remain faithful in a world increasingly drawn to spectacle.

A Strong Black Dominican Woman in America: Trials, Heritage, Faith, and Healing

My story as a strong Black Dominican woman in America is not a simple narrative of migration or ambition. It is a layered, textured, deeply human journey shaped by history, identity, and survival. It is the story of me as a woman who carries the weight of two worlds, the island that birthed me and the nation that tested me— and who learned to transform my pain into purpose through education, faith, culture, and creativity. My life became a living testament to the resilience of my ancestors, the power of Scripture, and the quiet strength found in solitude.

The Weight of Identity: A Black Dominican Woman in America

To be a Black Dominican woman in America is to live at the intersection of multiple identities, each carrying its own expectations and burdens. I am Afro-Latina, Caribbean, immigrant, woman, who is a little educated, and each identity shapes how the world sees me and how I see myself. In America, I was often misunderstood, miscategorized, or erased. People question my Blackness because I speak Spanish. They question my level Latinidad because of the color of my skin. They question my intelligence because of my accent. They question my belonging because of my heritage.

These daily microaggressions become a quiet storm that I must weather. Yet I stand firm, rooted in the knowledge that my identity is not a contradiction but a convergence, the product of Taíno survival, African endurance, and Spanish influence. My very existence is a historical truth that refuses to be simplified.

Trials and Tribulations: The Breaking Before the Rising

My trials are not small. They come in waves, financial hardship, family conflict, heartbreak, discrimination, loneliness, and the crushing pressure to succeed in a country that often feels indifferent to my struggle. I faced moments where the world seemed to collapse inward, where the weight of expectations suffocates me, where I felt unseen and unheard.

There are days when I wake up with heaviness in my chest, nights when I cried quietly so no one hears, Nights when even nightmares seem to return and seasons where isolation becomes my only companion. I experienced betrayal by people I had trusted, disappointment by opportunities that slipped away, and exhaustion from carrying responsibilities that were never meant to be mine alone.

Yet even in my lowest moments, something inside me refuses to die. A spark. A whisper. A memory of the women who came before me, my mother, my abuela, my ancestors who survived colonization, dictatorship, poverty, and migration. Their strength becomes my inheritance. I was always not on me; but in me.

Education as Liberation

Education has become my first weapon of survival. I became involved in all types of studies not just to earn degrees but to reclaim power in a world that had tried to diminish me. I read late into the night; I wrote papers through tears and pushed myself through exhaustion because I know that knowledge is a form of dominion. Now back then right after the pandemic I took courses on police and society, state and local government, criminal justice, criminal, criminology, Business Entrepreneurship, Business math, Business Law, Marketing and more. I refused to continue being a student of both the word and the world. In hopes to better understand all aspects of how this all connects and intersects.

In classrooms where sometimes I had been the only Black Latina, I had learned to speak with authority. In academic spaces that were not built for women like me, I carved out space anyway. My education became a shield against ignorance and a bridge toward opportunity. It also always teaches me discipline, critical thinking, and the ability to analyze my own life with clarity.

But education alone cannot heal the wounds life has carved into me. For that, I turned to something deeper. The study of the word in the Bible, its scriptures, verses, as well as their Bible stories.

The Bible as Anchor: Faith in the Midst of many Storms

When the world became too heavy, I turned to Scripture. The Bible became in many ways my refuge, not as a religious obligation, but as a lifeline. I read and studied all I could during my breaks from college classes. I read the Psalms when my heart ached, Proverbs when I needed wisdom, and the Gospels when I needed hope. I saw myself in the stories of women like:

• Hagar, who survived abandonment and found God in the wilderness.

• Ruth, who rebuilt her life through loyalty and resilience.

• Esther, who found courage in the face of danger.

• The Proverbs 31 woman, who worked with her hands, her mind, and her spirit.

These stories remind me that God has always used women who were overlooked, underestimated, or pushed to the margins. I began to understand that my suffering is not a sign of weakness but a pathway to purpose.

My Dominican Heritage: A History of Survival and Strength

My Dominican heritage becomes another pillar of my healing. I remember the rhythms of merengue and bachata that filled my childhood home, the smell of sofrito simmering on the stove, the stories of my ancestors who survived colonization, slavery, and dictatorship. I remember the resilience of Dominican women, the way they prayed loudly, worked tirelessly, and loved fiercely.

I carried the island in my bones. Its history became my reminder that came from a lineage of fighters, creators, and survivors. When I feel weak, I remember that my people have endured centuries of hardship and still found ways to dance, laugh, and praise God.

Talents as Therapy: Hair, Sewing, Crocheting, and Creation

My hands became instruments of healing. Through hair styling, I reconnect with the sacred tradition of Black women caring for one another. Braiding becomes meditation. Combing becomes prayer. Styling becomes a way to restore beauty, not just for others, but also for myself

Through sewing and crocheting, I learned patience, precision, and the quiet joy of creating something from nothing. Each stitch becomes a metaphor for my life, a reminder that broken pieces can be woven into something whole, something beautiful, something strong.

These talents are not hobbies; they are therapy. They are the ways I process pain, express creativity, and honor the women who taught in me and inherited these skills. Both on me and in me.

Isolation as Healing: The Wilderness Season

There are years when I isolated myself from everyone. Not out of bitterness, but out of necessity. I withdrew myself to protect my peace, to rebuild my spirit, to hear God's voice without interference. To watch church online, listens to Bible studies, meditate, journals, and sit in silence. The isolation I had begun to enact after my trials and tribulations. An exactment that I couldn't be threatened by during our years after the pandemic.

This isolation became my wilderness, the same kind of wilderness where God met Moses, Elijah, and Jesus. It is in this solitude that I confronted my wounds, released my anger, forgives myself for my level of tolerance, and learned to breathe again.

Isolation did not break me. It transformed me.

Rising Again: A Woman Reborn

By combining education, Scripture, heritage, creativity, and solitude, I rebuild myself from the inside out. I emerged stronger, wiser, and more grounded. I learned that healing is not a moment but a process, not a destination but a journey.

I became a woman who carries my culture with pride, my faith with conviction, and my talents with purpose. I became a woman who knows my worth, who honors my ancestors, who trusts God's timing, and who refuses to apologize for my strength.

My story became a testimony, a living example of how a Black Dominican woman in America can endure the worst trials and still rise with dignity, power, and grace.

A Mother at War: With Faith, With Identity, and with the Dominican dominion Fight Inside me FOR MY Children's Future

There are mothers who love quietly, and then there are mothers who go to war. Not with weapons, not with violence, but with a relentless, unbreakable spirit forged in struggle and sanctified by faith. This is my story of me as a mother who stands at the intersection of minority identity, limited resources, and overwhelming odds, yet refuses to bow. Me as a Black Dominican woman in America, or any woman of color as well as many Hispanic woman who carry the weight of two nations on our back and the future of our children in our hands. My life was and still is a battlefield, but my heart is a sanctuary. And every day, I fight.

My war is not fought on foreign soil. It is fought in classrooms where my children are underestimated, in workplaces where I am overlooked, in neighborhoods where opportunity is scarce, and in systems that were never designed for women like me. My battles stereotypes, discrimination, exhaustion, and fear, all while carrying the invisible armor of a mother's love. I know the world can be cruel, especially to children of color, especially to children of immigrants, especially to children who inherit the struggles of their ancestors. But I refuse to let the world swallow them whole. And brainwashed our next generation into this type of cultural society.

I fight with the weapons I have: My faith, my talents, my heritage, and my unshakable belief that God has a plan for my family.

A Minority Mother in a World That Underestimates Me:

Being a minority mother in America means living in a constant state of alertness. I know that one wrong move, one misunderstanding, one moment of vulnerability can cost me everything. It had already happened to me. Therefore, I navigate in a society that questions my intelligence, my accent, my culture, and my worth. I worked twice as hard for half the recognition. I stretched every dollar until it screamed. I sacrificed sleep, comfort, and dreams so my children can have a chance at a life I never truly had.

Yet I do not crumble. I stand tall despite being short, even when my knees were shaking. I smiled, even when my heart ached. I pushed forward, even when the world pushed back. My strength is not loud; it is steady. It is the strength of a woman who knows I cannot afford to break. Not in this generation, society, culture, and the pressure being placed on humanity as whole today.

Faith as my Armor: Jesus, the Son, and the Holy Spirit

What kept me standing is not luck or privilege, it is faith. Faith in Jesus the Son, who walked among the broken. Faith in the Holy Spirit, who whispers strength into weary bones. Faith in a God who sees my struggle and called me blessed, not forgotten.

I prayed over my children the way warriors sharpen their swords. I laid my hands on their heads and asks God to protect their minds, their perspectives, their mentalities. I prayed that they would see themselves not through the eyes of a world that limits them, but through the truth of Scripture that sets them free.

This verse became anthem. I prayed it into the air, into my home, into my children's spirits. I believed that the same God who parted seas and raised the dead can open doors for my children that no man can shut.

Dominican Blood, Dominican Fire

My Dominican heritage is not just a cultural identity, it is a source of power. I carried the island in my bones: the rhythm of merengue, the resilience of my ancestors, the pride of my people who survived colonization, dictatorship, and poverty. The Dominican flag is more than colors; it is a declaration of faith. "Dios, Patria, Libertad", God, Homeland, Freedom, is not just a motto. It is a spiritual inheritance.

I try to teach my children that they come from warriors, from survivors, from people who turned suffering into strength. I remind them that their Blackness is royal, their Dominican blood is sacred, and their identity is a gift, not a burden.

Talents as Tools: The Hands of a Provider

I may not have wealth, but I have so much talent, and talent is a currency of its own. My styles hair dressing with the precision of an artist, turning curls and coils into crowns. I sewed with the patience of my grandmother, stitching fabric into possibility. I crochet with the rhythm of prayer; each loop is a reminder that creation is a form of healing.

These talents are not hobbies; they are weapons. They are the tools that I will one day use to secure her children's future. My dreams of opening a business, building generational wealth, and showing my children that creativity can be a pathway to freedom.

There are wounds a family leaves on you that never fully close, only deepen with time. One of mine began the morning my father's girlfriend vanished. No warning, no goodbye, just gone. She took my little sister with her, the baby who shared our blood but not our fate. One day she was in the room next to mine, and next she was a ghost in a house full of unanswered questions.

My father had done to her exactly what he once did to my mother: pushed her to the edge until escape felt like the only form of survival. History didn't just repeat itself in my family, it recycled, reshaped, and returned with new victims. And this time, the prize was my little baby sister.

For decades, she lived only in my memory as a child I once held, a face I could barely recall, a name that felt like a prayer. I grew up wondering where she slept, what she looked like, whether she ever asked about us. I wondered if she knew she had siblings who never stopped searching for her.

Nearly thirty years passed before I found her—on a glowing screen, through the accidental mercy of modern technology. Instagram, of all places, became the bridge between a lifetime of silence and the truth I had been chasing since childhood. My hands shook when I typed the message. I didn't expect a miracle, but I hoped for something— recognition, curiosity, maybe even a sliver of connection.

What I received instead was a door slammed shut.

She wanted nothing to do with me. Not now, not ever. She told me she had her own life, her own father—the man who raised her, not the man who abandoned her. She believed we had lived some luxury life in America, far removed from the chaos she escaped. She saw us as strangers, not siblings. And in her eyes, reaching out to her was an intrusion, not a reunion.

Her rejection wasn't cruel; it was final. A boundary built from years of stories she had been told, and years of silence we had been forced to live with. She wasn't the little girl I remembered. She was a woman shaped by a different truth, one that didn't include me.

And yet, even in the sting of her refusal, there was something strangely comforting. After almost thirty years, I finally knew where she was. I finally saw her face. I finally understood the life she chose—or the life she was given. Technology gave me what life never did: an answer.

It wasn't the ending I wanted, but it was an ending. And sometimes, closure doesn't come wrapped in reunion or forgiveness. Sometimes it arrives quietly, through a screen, reminding you that even the people you lose can still be found—just not always in the way you hoped.

A Mother's War: Fought in Silence, Won in Faith

My war is not glamorous. It is fought in silence, in kitchens, in late-night prayers, in early-morning shifts, in tears I wipe before anyone sees. But it is a holy war, a war for peace, protection, and purpose.

I fight so that my children can grow up with minds unchained by fear, hearts unburdened by trauma, and spirits anchored in truth. I fight so they can walk boldly into rooms I was never allowed to enter. I fight so they can dream without limits.

And I believe, with every fiber of my being, that God will honor my fight.

A Mother's Legacy

In the end, my story is not one of defeat, but of divine resilience. I am a mother who goes to war not with violence, but with love. Not with weapons, but with prayer. Not with privilege, but with purpose. I am a Black Dominican woman in America, a minority with limited resources, but a daughter of the Most High God with unlimited faith.

My children will rise because I refused to fall.

My family will flourish because I refused to give up.

My legacy will shine because I carried my Dominican flag in one hand and the Bible in the other.

I am a mother at war, and I will win.

The Crisis of Trust in American Justice

Trust is the backbone of any justice system. Without it, laws lose their meaning, institutions lose their legitimacy, and people lose their sense of safety. In America today, that trust is unraveling, especially for minority communities, immigrant families, and mothers fighting for their children's survival. The justice system, which promises fairness and protection, often delivers fear, trauma, and betrayal instead. And for many, the question is no longer "How do we fix the system?" but "How do we survive it?"

Police Violence and the Shattering of Public Trust

Across the country, communities have watched unarmed people, disproportionately Black and brown, lose their lives in encounters that should never have turned deadly. These tragedies are not abstract statistics; they are videos burned into the national memory, funerals held too soon, and families left with grief instead of justice.

The fear is real. The trauma is generational. And the distrust is earned.

The Bible speaks directly to this kind of injustice:

"Woe to those who make unjust laws... to deprive the poor of their rights."

— Isaiah 10:1–2

When unarmed individuals are killed, when accountability is inconsistent, and when families are left with unanswered questions, the justice system becomes something to fear rather than trust.

ICE Enforcement and the Trauma of Family Separation

The crisis extends beyond policing. Immigration enforcement has intensified in ways that many families experience as persecution. According to NBC News, federal immigration officers have shot 11 people since September, often firing into cars, a tactic policing experts warn is dangerous and unnecessary. These incidents deepen the fear immigrant communities already carry.

Reports also show that immigration policies have upended lives, separated families, and eroded fundamental rights, with individuals transferred to countries where they face danger or detention. Many people believe these policies, especially family separation, have inflicted generational trauma on children who were taken from their parents at the border.

For a mother, there is no greater terror than losing her child. And for immigrant mothers, that terror is not hypothetical, it is lived reality.

Domestic Violence and the Criminalization of Survivors

Another hidden injustice lies within the walls of American homes. Domestic violence is a silent epidemic, and yet the justice system often fails the very women it claims to protect. Many mothers call the police for help, only to find themselves arrested instead of their abusers. Abusive partners manipulate the system, weaponizing their authority in the household to paint themselves as victims. Using their parent's resources or power or wealth.

As a result, countless women lose their homes, their children, and their stability, not because they failed as mothers, but because the system failed them.

These women are punished for surviving. They are punished for seeking help. They are punished for being vulnerable in a world that expects them to be strong.

The Bible commands:

"Defend the weak and the fatherless; uphold the cause of the poor and the oppressed."

— Psalm 82:3

Yet many mothers find themselves fighting alone.

Mothers Fighting for Their Children in a System That Fails Them

For minority mothers, especially Black, Latina, and immigrant women, the burden is even heavier. They must navigate racism, sexism, poverty, and systemic bias while trying to protect their children from a world that often sees them as threats rather than children.

They pray over their sons before they leave the house.

They teach their daughters how to survive encounters with authority. And how any man should be treating them with or without authority.

They carry generational trauma in their bodies and generational hope in their hearts.

These mothers are warriors, but even warriors grow tired.

Children Torn from Their Parents

Perhaps the most heartbreaking injustice is the separation of children from their parents, whether through immigration raids, domestic-violence misjudgments, or systemic failures in child protective services. Children are placed in foster care, detention centers, or shelters, while parents are left to fight impossible battles to reunite their families.

The trauma of separation leaves scars that last a lifetime. It violates the most sacred bond God created, the bond between parent and child.

Jesus Himself said:

"Let the little children come to me… for the kingdom of heaven belongs to such as these."

— Matthew 19:14

Yet in America today, children are often treated as collateral damage in political, legal, and bureaucratic systems. Even as Income like my mother-in-law only keeps fighting for mine for the benefits given by state and local governments like that of collecting thousands of dollars in food stamps, cash, and income tax returns and pandemic funds.

Faith as the Last Refuge

When justice fails, many turn to faith, not as an escape, but as a lifeline. They cling to the belief that God sees what the world ignores. They pray for protection, for fairness, for mercy, for change. They hold onto Scriptures like:

"The Lord is a refuge for the oppressed, a stronghold in times of trouble."

— Psalm 9:9

Faith becomes the only place where justice feels possible. Another important reason the Bible had become so important to me during both trauma and healing.

A Cry for True Justice

Trusting justice in America today is hard, painfully hard, for those who have been harmed by the very institutions meant to protect them. Police violence, immigration raids, family separations, and the criminalization of domestic-violence survivors all reveal a system in need of deep transformation.

But the cry for justice is not a cry of despair. It is a cry of hope, hope that America can become what it claims to be. Hope that the oppressed will be heard. I hope that families will be protected. I hope that children will be safe. Hope that justice will one day reflect the heart of God, who commands His people to "do justice, love mercy, and walk humbly" (Micah 6:8).

Until then, mothers, immigrants, survivors, and communities of color continue to fight, not because they trust the system, but because they believe their children deserve a world where justice is not a privilege, but a promise.

Carolina Santos: A Name Rooted in Identity, History, and Biblical Echo

My name was never just a name. It is a declaration, a prophecy, a spiritual fingerprint that followed me as a person long before I understood its weight. My name, Carolina Santos, carries history, culture, and faith woven into every syllable. It is Dominican in rhythm, biblical in meaning, and personal in the way it has shaped the woman I have become.

Carolina, A Name of Strength and Stewardship

The name Carolina comes from the Latin Carolus, meaning "free woman," "strong woman," or "woman of courage." It is a name tied to leadership, resilience, and the ability to endure. In many cultures, Carolina is associated with queens, warriors, and women who carry themselves with quiet authority. But for me, the meaning goes deeper.

To be a Carolina is to be a woman who survives what should have broken me.

To be a Carolina is to walk through fire and come out refined.

To be a Carolina is to embody the biblical truth:

"She is clothed with strength and dignity, and I laughed without fear of the future."

— Proverbs 31:25

The Dominican Republic is full of women like this, women who hold families together, who work with their hands, who pray with fire, who carry generations on their backs. The name Carolina fits into that lineage naturally. It is a Dominican woman's name not because of geography, but because of spirit.

In the Bible, God repeatedly chooses people whose names reflect their calling.

- Sarah, mother of nations

- Deborah, the bee, the warrior-judge

- Hannah, grace

- Mary, beloved

Carolina stands among these names as a reminder that identity is not accidental. It is intentional. It is prophetic. It is a calling to live boldly, freely, and with purpose.

Santos, A Name of Holiness and Heritage

If Carolina is the strength, Santos is the sanctification.

The surname Santos literally means "saints," "holy ones," or "those set apart."

It is a name rooted in Spanish and Portuguese tradition, carried across oceans through colonization, migration, and faith. In the Dominican Republic, Santos is a common surname, not because Dominicans are perfect, but because Dominican identity is deeply tied to spirituality, Catholic tradition, and the belief that God's presence is woven into everyday life.

The name Santos carries biblical weight. In Scripture, "saints" refers not to flawless people, but to those chosen, protected, and set apart by God:

"To the saints and faithful brothers and sisters in Christ…"

— Colossians 1:2

A saint is someone God refuses to abandon.

Someone He calls His own.

Someone He rescues repeatedly. Same way he had repeatedly rescued me.

When I carry the name Santos, I carry the reminder that God has marked my life with purpose, even when I didn't see it, even when I didn't feel it, even when I was walking through darkness.

The Dominican Connection: A Name That Carries a Nation

Together, Carolina Santos is a name that sounds like home, like merengue on a Sunday morning, like my grandmother's prayers, like the Dominican flag waving in the heat of July. Dominican names often carry a blend of African, Taíno, and Spanish influence, and Santos is one of the clearest examples of that colonial and spiritual fusion.

Dominicans are a people shaped by survival, slavery, colonization, dictatorship, migration, poverty, and resilience. The name Santos reflects that history. It is a reminder that even in suffering, Dominicans have always held onto faith. Churches, altars, rosaries, and prayers have been woven into Dominican culture for centuries.

To be a Dominican with the last name Santos is to carry the legacy of a people who refused to lose their faith even when everything else was taken from them.

The Biblical Connection: A Name That Speaks of Calling

When you put my two names together, Carolina Santos, you get a meaning that feels almost prophetic:

"A strong, free woman set apart by God."

This is not just a definition. It is a declaration.

It is the story of a woman who have survived premature birth, family separation, violence, trauma, and chaos, yet still stands. It is the story of a woman who has been protected by God in moments where survival made no sense. It is the story of a woman whose life has been spared repeatedly, not by luck, but by grace. The Grace of the God Almighty the Most High.

The Bible says:

"Before I formed you in the womb, I knew you."

— Jeremiah 1:5

My name reflects that truth.

My survival reflects that truth.

My story reflects that truth.

A Name That Became my Testimony

Carolina Santos is not just a name, it is a testimony.

It is the testimony of a Dominican woman who has walked through fire and came out with purpose.

It is the testimony of a woman whose identity was and is rooted in strength and holiness.

It is the testimony of a woman who carries my ancestors, my culture, and my God in every step I take.

My name is My Story.

My story is my strength.

And my strength is my calling.

My father's Name "José de Jesús": Dominican Identity, Biblical Legacy, and the Weight of his name

Names carry history. They carry culture, memory, and spiritual inheritance. Some names are simple labels, but others are declarations, reminders of where a person comes from and what they were born into. My father's name, José de Jesús, is one of those names. It is a name that echoes across the Dominican Republic, across Scripture, and across generations of faith. It is a name that carries both earthly identity and divine symbolism.

The First Name: José, A Name Rooted in Survival and Purpose

The name José is the Spanish form of Joseph, one of the most significant names in the Bible. Joseph appears twice in Scripture as a man chosen to protect, provide, and endure.

Joseph of Genesis

- Sold by his brothers

- Thrown into a pit

- Imprisoned unjustly

- Yet rose to power in Egypt

- Saved nations from famine

His story is one of betrayal, resilience, and divine purpose. Joseph's life teaches that even when people intend harm, God can turn it into destiny:

"You meant evil against me, but God meant it for good."

— Genesis 50:20

Joseph of the Gospels

- Earthly father of Jesus

- A man of humility, obedience, and quiet strength

- Protected Mary and Jesus from danger

- Guided his family through uncertainty

This Joseph teaches that leadership is not always loud, sometimes it is steady, faithful, and unseen.

When a Dominican man carries the name José, he carries both legacies:

the survivor and the protector,

the dreamer and the provider,

the man who endures and the man who obeys.

In Dominican culture, the name José is everywhere, in families, in history, in the streets named after saints. It reflects the island's deep Catholic roots and the belief that names carry spiritual covering. To be named José is to be tied to a biblical lineage of men who carried responsibility on their shoulders and faith in their hearts.

The Last Name: De Jesús, A Name That Speaks of Identity and Calling

The surname de Jesús literally means "of Jesus."

It is a name that does not whisper faith, it declares it.

In Spanish-speaking cultures, especially in the Caribbean and Latin America, surnames like de Jesús, de la Cruz, del Rosario, and Santos reflect centuries of Catholic influence. They are reminders that faith was not just practiced, it was woven into identity.

But de Jesús is different. It is intimate. It is bold. It is a name that places a person in direct connection with Christ.

To carry the name de Jesús is to carry:

- A reminder of divine protection

- A symbol of spiritual inheritance

- A connection to the story of salvation

- A declaration that one's identity is tied to something greater

In the Bible, Jesus is the center of everything, the fulfillment of prophecy, the embodiment of grace, the bridge between humanity and God. A surname like de Jesús carries that weight, that hope, that spiritual proximity.

The Dominican Connection: Faith, Culture, and Colonial Legacy

In the Dominican Republic, names like José de Jesús are common not because Dominicans are perfect, but because Dominican identity is deeply tied to faith. The island's history is marked by:

- Catholic tradition

- Spanish influence

- African spirituality

- Indigenous resilience

The Dominican Republic is a place where people pray loudly, worship passionately, and call on God in every crisis. Faith is not a Sunday ritual, it is a survival tool, a cultural inheritance, a way of life.

A Dominican man named José de Jesús carries the weight of that culture. His name reflects:

- The island's religious history

- The blending of Spanish naming traditions with Caribbean identity

• The belief that God's presence is part of everyday life

Dominicans often say "Si Dios quiere" (God willing) or "Gracias a Dios" (Thank God) because faith is woven into language itself. A name like de Jesús fits naturally into this worldview, a reminder that even in struggle, God is nearby.

The Biblical Echo: A Name That Speaks of Purpose

When you put the two names together, José de Jesús, the meaning becomes powerful:

"Joseph of Jesus"

or

"A protector connected to Christ."

This combination mirrors the biblical Joseph, who protected Jesus as a child. It also reflects the Joseph of Genesis, who saved his family from destruction.

My father's name carries themes of:

• Protection

• Provision

• Sacrifice

• Faith

- Calling

It is a name that suggests a man who stands between danger and the people he loves. A man who carries responsibility. A man whose identity is tied to something sacred.

A Name That Becomes Legacy

For me, as his daughter, the name José de Jesús becomes part of my own story. It shapes my heritage, my identity, and my understanding of where I came from. It connects me to:

- Dominican culture

- Biblical history

- Generational faith

- Spiritual purpose

My father's name is not just a label, it is a legacy. It is a reminder that my roots are both earthly and divine, both Caribbean and biblical, both cultural and spiritual.

Absence, Identity, and the Day My Mother Finally Arrived

There are absences that feel like shadows, always present, always following, always reminding you of what you never had. Growing up in America without a mother that was one of those shadows. It shaped the way I understood love, family, and myself. It shaped the way I moved through the world, always searching for something I could not name. And it shaped the way I imagined the woman who gave me life, even though I had never seen her face. Or more like I don't remember or face or what she looked like.

For most people, a mother is the first image they remember. For me, she was a blank space. A story told in fragments. If ever told, my father spoke about her good or bad. A voice I could not recall. A presence I felt only through the ache of her absence. I grew up knowing I had a mother somewhere in the Dominican Republic; but not knowing what she looked like, not her eyes, not her smile, not the shape of her hands. I grew up with a twin sister beside me, but without the woman who carried us both into existence.

America became the place where I learned to survive without her. I learned to navigate childhood, adolescence, and adulthood without a mother-shaped hole in my life. I watched other girls braid their mother's hair, borrow their mother's clothes, cry into their mother's arms, and I learned to swallow the envy quietly. I learned to be strong because I had no choice. I learned to mother myself because no one else could fill that role.

But even strength has its limits. Even independence has its breaking points. And even the deepest wounds carry a longing that time cannot erase.

For years, my mother existed only in imagination. I pictured her as a silhouette, a mystery, a woman suspended between the Dominican Republic and the life I was building in the United States. I wondered if she thought of me. I wondered if she prayed for me. I wondered if she remembered the shape of my face the way I longed to know hers.

Then one ordinary day, a day like any other, after work, tired and ready to go home, everything changed.

My phone rang. It was my twin sister. Her voice was urgent, trembling, the kind of tone that makes your heart drop before you even hear the words. She told me there was an emergency. She told me to meet her at the airport in New Jersey. She told me to arrival immediately, or as soon as I could make it the drive was about nearly 5 hours away from my job, but I had made it.

I didn't ask questions. I didn't need details. Something in me, instinct, spirit, blood, told me this moment was bigger than fear, bigger than confusion, bigger than anything I had ever faced. I thought my sister was planning to leave the country. Since she had already left the state, she moved nearly 5 hours away sporadically. I drove with my heart pounding, my mind racing, my hands shaking on the steering wheel. I didn't know what was waiting for me on the other side of that airport door, but I felt the weight of destiny pressing on my chest.

When I arrived, the air felt different, heavy, electric, sacred. My sister stood there, eyes wide, face pale, as if I had seen a ghost. And in a way, I had.

Because standing beside me was a woman I had never seen before. A woman whose face was unfamiliar, but whose presence hit me like a tidal wave. A woman who looked at me with eyes that mirrored my own. A woman whose hands trembled the way mine did. A woman who carried the same blood, the same history, the same story.

It was my mother.

After decades of absence, after years of imagining her face, after a lifetime of wondering if I would ever see her again, she was standing in front of me, real and breathing, fresh off a flight from the Dominican Republic. A woman I had lived without for so long suddenly existed in flesh and bone, close enough to touch. And I no longer had to wonder what she looked like. Or imagine what is now directly in front of me.

The moment felt unreal. My mind struggled to catch up with my heart. I didn't know whether to cry, to run, to collapse, or to speak. All I knew was that something inside me had been empty for years, shifted. Filled. Softened.

Meeting her was not just a reunion. It was a resurrection.

A part of me that had been buried came back to life.

Growing up without a mother had taught me resilience but meeting her taught me something deeper: that some stories take decades to unfold, that some wounds take years to heal, and that some reunions happen only when God decides the time is right.

I had spent my entire life not knowing what my mother looked like. And then, in one moment, I saw her, not just with my eyes, but with my spirit. I saw the woman who carried me. I saw the woman whose absence shaped me. I saw the woman whose presence, even after all these years, still mattered.

That day in the New Jersey airport there was not just a meeting. It was the beginning. A reminder that even the most broken stories can find their way back to wholeness. A reminder that God's timing is mysterious but perfect. A reminder that loves, even when delayed, can still arrive.

And for the first time in my life, I understood what it meant to investigate the face of the woman who gave me mine.

on Nails, Womanhood, and the Unexpected Path to Healing

There are parts of a woman's body that the world teaches her to overlook, small details that seem insignificant until life forces her to pay attention. Nails are one of those details. Most people think of nails as decoration, as vanity, as something women do "for fun." But nails are more than polish and color. They are literally bones, extensions of the body's structure, a physical reminder that even the smallest parts of us deserve care, attention, and protection.

For me, learning this wasn't just biology. It was personal. It was emotional. It was spiritual.

Growing up, I never thought much about nails beyond the way they looked. I admired women who had the time and money to sit in a salon, to let a nail tech shape their hands into something beautiful. But I didn't grow up with that luxury as part of self-care; but more of a gift or present. I didn't grow up with the kind of stability that allowed selfcare appointments or pampering on a weekly basis. My life was survival, movement, chaos, and responsibility. Beauty was something I admired from afar, not something I believed I deserved. But something that just simply had to be done as my father would say to be a lady.

But as I got older, I learned something that changed the way I saw myself: nails are bone. They are part of the body's structure, part of what protects us, part of what grows even when life feels stagnant. And like any bone, they can weaken if neglected. They can break if ignored. They can become damaged if we don't take care of them.

That realization hit me harder than I expected.

Because it wasn't just about nails, it was about me.

I had spent years taking care of everyone else. Years putting my needs last. Years of believing that self-care was a luxury I couldn't afford. But the truth was that I had been neglecting parts of myself that needed attention, love, and healing. My nails became a metaphor for my life: small, overlooked, but essential.

When I couldn't afford a nail tech, I felt that familiar sting of lack, the reminder that I didn't have what other women had. But instead of letting that feeling defeat me, something inside me shifted. I decided to learn. I decided to teach myself what I couldn't pay for. I decided to become my own nail tech.

What started as a financial necessity became a form of therapy.

I bought cheap tools. I watched videos. I practiced on myself, on friends, on anyone who would let me. My hands shook at first, but with time, they steadied. I learned how to shape, buff, file, and polish. I learned how to repair damage, how to strengthen weak nails, how to create beauty from nothing.

And somewhere in that process, I realized I wasn't just fixing nails —

I was fixing myself.

Every stroke of the file felt like smoothing out a rough part of my past.

Every layer of polish felt like reclaiming a piece of my identity.

Every moment spent caring for my hands felt like a reminder that I deserved care too.

Nail care became a ritual, a quiet moment where I could breathe, focus, and reconnect with myself. It became a way to slow down in a life that had always demanded speed. It became a way to honor the parts of me that had been ignored for too long.

And it became healing.

Not the loud, dramatic kind of healing people talk about in movies, but the slow, steady, intimate kind, the kind that happens in small moments, in quiet rooms, with my own hands doing the work. The kind that teaches me that I can create beauty even when life has tried to break me.

Learning to do my own nails taught me that healing doesn't always come from big gestures or expensive treatments. Sometimes healing comes from the simple act of caring for yourself in ways I was never taught to. Sometimes healing comes from reclaiming the parts of me that were neglected. Sometimes healing comes from realizing that even the smallest bones in my body deserve love. Like that of my own nailcare.

Today, when I look at my hands, I don't just look at nails.

I see survival.

I see growth.

I see a woman who learned to take care of herself when no one else could.

I see healing, slow, steady, and beautifully earned.

The Dominion of Healing: Women Rising Through Heritage, Faith, and Sisterhood

Across generations and continents, women have carried the quiet power to heal—first themselves, then their families, and ultimately their communities. This healing has never been limited to medicine or miracles; it has always lived in the everyday practices of culture, faith, creativity, and connection. For many women, especially those shaped by the rich rhythms of Dominican heritage, healing is a tapestry woven from the threads of ancestry, Scripture, talent, and the God-given dominion placed within them. It is a journey of reclaiming identity, nurturing the spirit, and lifting one another up in a world that often tries to tear them down.

Healing begins with remembering who we are and where we come from. Dominican women—past and present—have always carried a legacy of resilience. Centuries ago, women in the Dominican Republic gathered in courtyards, kitchens, and open fields to share stories, braid hair, sing songs, teach each other skills, and pass down wisdom. They worshiped together, prayed together, and survived together. Their communion was not just social; it was spiritual. It was a living example of Proverbs' reminder that "iron sharpens iron," and a reflection of the dominion God gave His daughters: the authority to nurture, to build, to restore, and to stand firm in faith.

Today, that same dominion still lives in women, though the world around them has changed. Modern life offers new tools—education, technology, global connection—but it also brings new distractions and new wounds. Many women now carry trauma silently, scrolling through social media where comparison, criticism, and competition often replace community. Instead of gathering to uplift one another, too many gather to tear each other down. Instead of celebrating each other's gifts, too many feel pressured to hide their own. Yet the path to healing remains the same as it was for our ancestors: returning to God, returning to our roots, and returning to each other.

Healing is found in embracing the beauty God placed within us—not just physical beauty, but the beauty of our talents, our creativity, and our purpose. A woman who styles hair is not just doing a job; she is practicing an art that has connected women for centuries. A woman who sews or crochets is not just making clothing; she is stitching together culture, memory, and identity. A woman who sings or dances is not just performing; she is releasing emotion, honoring her ancestors, and praising her Creator. A woman who exercises is not just strengthening her body; she is reclaiming her temple. A woman who reads the Bible is not just studying; she is feeding her spirit and aligning her life with God's Word.

Each of these practices becomes a form of healing when done with intention. They remind women that they are more than their pain, more than their past, and more than the world's expectations. They remind women that God placed dominion within them—not to dominate others, but to rise above fear, shame, and trauma. Dominion means authority over one's mind, one's choices, one's healing, and one's future. It means living in the Word, not just reading it. It means walking with Christ, not just knowing His name. It means using every gift—cultural, spiritual, creative—to build a life rooted in purpose.

But healing is not meant to be done alone. Women are strongest when they walk together. When women gather in communion, something sacred happens burdens become lighter, wisdom becomes richer, and healing becomes deeper. Just as Dominican women once shared stories under the shade of palm trees, today's women can share testimonies in living rooms, churches, community centers, and online spaces built for encouragement rather than destruction. When women teach each other skills—whether it's sewing, cooking, budgeting, studying Scripture, or navigating motherhood—they are continuing a tradition that has sustained generations.

And when women worship together, pray together, and study the Bible together, they create a spiritual force that breaks generational curses and builds generational blessings. This is the kind of sisterhood that transforms families, strengthens communities, and shapes the future. This is the kind of unity that teaches daughters how to love themselves, teaches sons how to honor women, and teaches the world what true dominion looks like.

The truth is simple: women were never meant to heal in isolation. God designed women to be nurturers, connectors, and builders. Dominican heritage teaches us that community is a lifeline. The Bible teaches us that fellowship is a command. And life teaches us that healing becomes powerful when shared.

So today, women are called to return to what has always made them strong: their culture, their faith, their talents, their beauty, and their sisterhood. They are called to lift each other up instead of tearing each other down. They are called to educate themselves and one another—not just academically, but spiritually, emotionally, and creatively. They are called to raise families with wisdom, to build futures with intention, and to walk in the dominion God placed within them from the beginning.

When women rise together, healing becomes unstoppable. And when women walk with Christ—hand in hand, heart to heart—the world around them begins to heal too.

Dominican Faith Forged in Fire: Healing Through History, Scripture, and Truth

The island of Hispaniola, our home, our inheritance, was the first to bleed under European conquest. The Taíno people, our ancestors, were the first to be enslaved, the first to resist, and the first to be nearly erased. But God does not forget the cries of the oppressed. From the moment Columbus stepped onto our soil, the battle for our soul began. And yet, we are still here.

History of Dominican Republic and Hispaniola – The Island of Firsts reminds us that our land was the birthplace of resistance. The Haitian Revolution, the Dominican independence, the revolts, the uprisings, all of it was soaked in blood and prayer. We were not just fighting colonizers. We were fighting to reclaim our God-given dominion.

The Bible says in **Psalm 147:3**, *"He heals the brokenhearted and binds up their wounds."* That is the Dominican story. We are a people wounded by slavery, by dictatorship, by poverty, by migration, but we are also a people healed by faith, by family, by music, by culture, by God.

Today, Dominicans face new battles: racism in foreign lands, corruption at home, generational trauma, and spiritual confusion. But our history is not just pain, it is prophecy. The same God who parted the Red Sea for Moses is the God who parted the chains of Trujillo's tyranny. The same God who raised up Esther to save her people is raising up Dominican women today, bold, brown, braided, and brilliant, to speak truth, to heal, to lead.

Romans 8:28 says, *"And we know that in all things God works for the good of those who love him."* Even the colonization. Even the exile. Even the silence. God is working. Our healing is not just personal, it is national. It is spiritual. It is generational.

We are the children of the Taíno, the Africans, the Spanish, and the Spirit. We are the island of firsts, yes, but we are also the island of faith. And that faith is our weapon. That faith is our healing. That faith is our dominion.

Stewards of the First Island: How Dominican History Shapes Our Faith and Healing

Before the world knew the Caribbean, before maps had names, before colonizers planted flags, **the Taíno people of Quisqueya, the Dominican Republic, were already living as stewards of the first island touched by European conquest**. Hispaniola was the cradle of the New World, the first place where the soil felt the weight of colonization, the first place where Indigenous people were enslaved, and the first place where African people were forced into bondage.

This means something important:

Dominicans were here first. Dominicans suffered first. Dominicans resisted first.

And this history is not just a timeline, it is a spiritual inheritance.

The Taíno: Guardians Before the Arrival of Puerto Ricans

The Taíno people lived across the Caribbean, but **Hispaniola was their heartland**, their largest population, their political center, and the first place where their world was shattered.

When the Spanish arrived in 1492, the Taíno of Quisqueya were the first to face enslavement, disease, and forced labor. They were the first to be taken into mines, the first to be forced into encomiendas, the first to be broken, and the first to rebel.

Puerto Rico (Borikén) was colonized **after** Hispaniola. The systems of slavery, violence, and exploitation used in Puerto Rico were **copied** from what the Spanish had already done in the Dominican Republic. The Taíno of Quisqueya were the blueprint, the first victims, the first fighters, the first martyrs.

So when we say Dominicans were here before Puerto Ricans, it is not arrogance, it is historical truth. **Our ancestors were already carrying the weight of colonization before Puerto Rico even entered the story.**

Dominicans Were Also Among the First Enslaved People in the Americas

Long before the United States existed, long before Puerto Ricans migrated to New York in the 1900s, **enslaved people from Hispaniola were already being transported into early American colonies**.

The Spanish used the Caribbean as a human pipeline. Enslaved Taíno and African people from the Dominican Republic were taken to:

- early Spanish settlements in Florida
- early tobacco farms in the American Southeast
- and later, even to Hawaii's sugar plantations under contract labor systems

Dominicans, through their Indigenous and African ancestors, were **already present in the earliest forced labor systems of the Americas**.

So when Puerto Ricans arrived in the 20th century, Dominicans had already been part of the American story for centuries, not by choice, but by chains.

A People Forged in Fire: How History Shapes Dominican Faith

Our history is not gentle. It is not soft. It is not clean.

It is **raw**, **bloody**, and **holy**.

Because every time the world tried to erase us, God wrote us back into the story.

The Bible says:

"The stone the builders rejected has become the cornerstone.", Psalm 118:22

That is the Dominican story.

We were the first to be broken, but we became the foundation of the Caribbean. We were the first to be enslaved, but we became the first to rebel. We were the first to lose everything, but we became the first to rise again.

Our suffering is not meaningless, it is prophetic.

Healing Through Faith: What Our Ancestors Teach Us Today

Dominicans today carry the trauma of:

- colonization
- colorism
- migration
- poverty
- dictatorship
- and spiritual disconnection

But we also carry the **faith** of a people who survived the impossible.

The Taíno believed in a Creator. The Africans brought a deep spiritual strength. The Spanish brought Christianity. And out of that collision came a people who know how to pray through pain.

Romans 5:3–4 says:

"Suffering produces endurance, endurance produces character, and character produces hope."

This is why Dominicans are resilient. This is why Dominicans heal. This is why Dominicans rise.

Our history forged our faith. Our faith fuels our healing. And our healing becomes our testimony.

Why This Matters Now

In a world where Dominicans face:

- racism abroad
- corruption at home
- identity confusion
- generational trauma
- and spiritual warfare

We must remember:

We were stewards before we were slaves. We were a people before we were a colony. We were chosen before we were broken.

God has always been with us.

Just as He heard the cries of the Israelites in Egypt, He heard the cries of the Taíno in Quisqueya. Just as He walked with Daniel in the lions' den, He walked with the enslaved Africans in the cane fields. Just as He restored Israel, He is restoring the Dominican people today.

Conclusion: A People Rising

Dominicans are not an accident of history. We are a people forged in fire, protected by God, and rising with purpose.

Our ancestors were the first stewards of the Caribbean. Our people were among the first enslaved in the Americas. And today, we are among the first to reclaim our identity, our faith, and our healing.

Dios, Patria, Libertad is not just a motto. It is a prophecy.

And we are living it.

THE ISLAND OF FIRSTS: How Dominican History, Faith, and Resilience Prepare Us for National Freedom

The Dominican Republic is not just another Caribbean nation. It is the **first chapter** of the Americas, the first soil touched by colonization, the first battlefield of resistance, the first classroom, the first hospital, the first church, the first rebellion, the first mixing of worlds, the first suffering, and the first hope.

Everything that happened in the New World happened **first** in Quisqueya.

And that matters.

Because a people who endure first are also the people God strengthens first.

A people who bleed first are the people God heals first.

A people who are broken first are the people God raises first.

This is the Dominican story.

The First Stewards of the First Island

Before the world knew the Caribbean, the **Taíno of Quisqueya** were already here, cultivating the land, naming the mountains, fishing the rivers, honoring the Creator. They were the **largest and most advanced Taíno population** in the region.

They were the first:

- to build organized chiefdoms
- to develop agricultural systems
- to create spiritual practices rooted in community
- to welcome outsiders with peace

They were the **original stewards** of the island long before colonizers or neighboring islands entered the story.

When the Spanish arrived, the Taíno of Quisqueya were the **first Indigenous people enslaved** in the Americas. The first to be forced into mines. The first to be taken as captives to other colonies. The first to die in mass numbers. The first to rebel.

Their suffering became the blueprint for the entire hemisphere.

The First Colony, First City, First Church, First Hospital, First University

Hispaniola became the **prototype** for the Americas.

The Dominican Republic was the first place where Europeans built:

- **the first city** (Santo Domingo)
- **the first cathedral**
- **the first hospital**
- **the first university**
- **the first court system**
- **the first roads and ports**

This means the Dominican Republic was the **first center of education, medicine, religion, and government** in the New World.

While the rest of the Americas were forests and tribal lands, Quisqueya was already a **capital of learning and administration**.

Dominicans were the first to be taught European education, and the first to resist it when it became a tool of oppression.

The First Enslaved and the First Liberators

Dominicans, Indigenous and African, were among the **first enslaved people transported across the Americas**, including into early U.S. territories.

Before the United States existed, Dominican bodies were already being exploited in:

- Florida
- Georgia
- early Spanish settlements
- sugar plantations across the Caribbean

But we were also the **first to rebel**.

The first maroon communities. The first uprisings. The first organized resistance against European rule.

Our ancestors were not passive victims, they were warriors.

The First to Blend Worlds and Survive the Collision

Dominicans became the first people in the Americas to embody:

- Indigenous Taíno blood
- African strength
- Spanish language and religion

We were the first multicultural, multiracial society in the hemisphere.

This mixture was not peaceful, it was born from violence, trauma, and survival. But God has a way of turning ashes into beauty.

Genesis 50:20 says: *"You meant evil against me, but God meant it for good."*

That is the Dominican identity. We are the product of tragedy transformed into purpose.

The First to Declare Themselves a Free People

Dominican independence was not just political, it was spiritual.

When the founders wrote **Dios, Patria y Libertad**, they were declaring:

- God is our source
- The land is our inheritance
- Freedom is our destiny

We were the first Caribbean nation to embed **God** directly into our national identity.

The Bible was placed at the center of our flag, not as decoration, but as covenant.

John 8:32: *"And you will know the truth, and the truth will set you free."*

Dominicans believed that truth was not just a verse, it was a prophecy.

The Weight We Carry Today

Dominicans today face:

- corruption
- poverty
- colorism
- migration trauma
- spiritual confusion
- generational wounds

But we also carry something stronger:

the memory of being first.

First to endure. First to learn. First to resist. First to rebuild. First to rise.

Our resilience is not accidental, it is inherited.

Our faith is not borrowed, it is forged.

Our identity is not fragile, it is ancient.

Dios, Patria y Libertad: The Prophecy of Our Healing

Dominicans are entering a new era, one where our history becomes our weapon, our faith becomes our medicine, and our resilience becomes our liberation.

Dios, because God has always walked with us through genocide, slavery, dictatorship, and diaspora. **Patria**, because the land remembers every prayer, every rebellion, every drop of blood. **Libertad**, because freedom is not just political; it is spiritual, emotional, generational.

The same God who healed Israel after exile is healing Dominicans after centuries of trauma.

The same God who restored Jerusalem is restoring Quisqueya.

The same God who turned slaves into leaders is turning Dominicans into a nation of purpose.

Conclusion: A Nation Rising Again

Dominicans were the first to suffer, but we will also be the first to rise.

We were the first to be broken, but we will be the first to be healed.

We were the first to be enslaved, but we will be the first to walk in true freedom.

Our history is not a wound, it is a prophecy.

And **Dios, Patria y Libertad** is not just a motto. It is the key that will finally set us free.

For "Anti-So-Called History" by Carolina Santos, featuring a complex blend of Dominican nationalism, religious iconography, and placeholder text. The central message is one of spiritual and national reclamation, suggesting that the Dominican Republic is a nation defined by a divine contract. This is anchored by the large Dominican flag waving at the top and the figure of Jesus Christ emerging in the background, which reinforces the subtitle's claim of "A Nation Under God" and a "Dominican Covenant." Below this, a vibrant colonial scene depicts people in traditional dress dancing and gathering at a harbor with old sailing ships, grounding the book's high-level theological themes in the historical and cultural life of the island's inhabitants.

The book cover for "Anti-So-Called History" by Carolina Santos serves as a visual manifesto for a providentialist and revisionist interpretation of Dominican identity, centered on the belief that the nation exists under a literal divine mandate. At its heart lies the Dominican Coat of Arms, featuring an open Bible set to John 8:32 ("The truth shall make you free"), which the author links to her title to suggest that "the truth" of the nation's origin has been obscured by mainstream historical narratives. This "Dominican Covenant" refers to the spiritual oath of the Trinitarios, the founding fathers who established the country under the invocation of the Holy Trinity, positioning the Republic's sovereignty not merely as a political achievement, but as a sacred contract with God. The imagery reinforces this by flanking the central cross with Lady Justice, representing a demand for moral and historical rectitude, and a woman in a "Flag Dress" standing beside a basket of tropical bounty, which roots this high-level theology in the physical land and the everyday cultural life of the people. By labeling mainstream accounts as "So-Called History," Santos signals a journey to reclaim a heritage where the national motto—Dios, Patria, Libertad— is treated as an active, binding prophecy rather than a symbolic relic, arguing that the nation's ultimate "Liberty" is dependent upon returning to its "God" and "Fatherland" roots.